Translations from World Literature

TRANSLATIONS FROM WORLD LITERATURE

WITH AN INTRODUCTION AND NOTES

EDITED BY

LELA G. JGERENAIA
ANTHONY S. KLINE

CONTENTS

―――――

GEORGIAN

ACKNOWLEDGMENTS

This work would not be possible without the effort and support of my friends and colleagues. I would like to thank Marsin Alshamary for her administrative assistance, Genevieve Goldleaf for designing the book cover, and Gissell F. Castellon for developing an online resource for this compilation. Thanks to the Wellesley College Departments of Russian Studies, Classics, German, French, and Anthropology for their financial and editorial support.

Lela Jgerenaia

PREFACE

The idea for this compilation was conceived, like many great ideas, over a cup of tea while discussing poetry with friends. As I shared my translations of Georgian poetry with my friends, which I did gradually as I feel that poetry is quite personal, I realized that these works were not meant for only Georgians or myself, but for everyone. Vazha Pshavela's work had a significant impact on me. He lived in the mountainous region of Georgia during the nineteenth century, where war and revenge were the common rule of people's daily lives. He protested the brutality of what he saw. He appreciated the beauty of nature and it was his main inspiration, as well as life itself with its injustices. What struck me in reading other translated works were the eloquent illustrations of cultural differences as well as the profoundly universal nature of the common themes. Vazha Pshavela's "Why was I Made as a Human?" asks a question that has been echoed since the dawn of human consciousness. This work is as relevant today as it was in nineteenth century Georgia. As my friends and I shared more of our translated works with each other, I became more interested in international literary translations. Though collections of translated works from a single language or author abounded, there were few with works from different cultures and languages. There were certainly no such compilations available in my native Georgian language! Thus, this work was inspired by my own personal love of poetry, the enthusiasm of other literary translators in sharing their own works, and the joy of understanding and comparing different cultures through literature and poetry. I hope you enjoy reading this compilation as much as I enjoyed putting it together to share with you.

INTRODUCTION

This book presents short stories, songs and poems translated from 17 different languages. Some of the works refer to culturally specific items or topics. For some of the more difficult to understand translations, the translators offer a brief background that will make it easier for you the reader to fully understand the works within their cultural context.

Host and Guest by Vazha-Pshavela

Host and guest is a poem based on the Georgian rule of hospitality. Hospitability is sacred. Hosts usually sacrifice their own comfort for that of their guest. It is considered a great dishonor to the host and his family if their guest is captured or harmed in any way while under the care of the host.

The poem is about two warring tribes, Kists and Khevsurs. Kists are people in the Caucasus from the "VeiNakh" tribes. "VeiNakh" means "our people." This is what Chechens, Ingush and Kist people call themselves to differentiate themselves from other Caucasians in the mountainous regions. Kists speak a dialect of Chechen-Ingush language. They had close contact with Georgian tribes. Khevsurs are a Georgian tribe living in the mountainous region of Georgia. Both tribes still have very peculiar traditions and cultures, which differentiate them from other Georgians.

According to custom in the mountainous regions of nineteenth century Georgia, the victors in battle would sever the right hand of their slain enemies. The severed right hands of one's defeated foes would be brought back to the

victor's home village and hung on the front of the house. The more right hands collected and displayed, the greater the warrior's reputation for courage and valor.

There are following main characters in the poem:

Jockola – Kist tribe member, husband of Aghaza
Zviadauri –Khevsur tribe member
Aghaza – Kist tribe member; wife of Jockola
Musa – the leader of Kist tribe

Lela Jgerenaia

Arabic Poetry

Arabic poetry is written meticulously with particular attention given to meter and rhyme. Traditional poetry, such as the poem from *Ali IbnAbiTalib* is written in two columns that are designed to have identical meters, rhythms, and rhymes. The two column style of poetry is very popular in Arabic and we have tried our best to conserve it. The translations we could not fit into two columns, because the English equivalent to the Arabic did not have equal rhyme and meter. Therefore, each line in Arabic (spread across the two columns) is the equivalent of two lines in English. As free verse became more popular in the Arab world and the rules restricting poetry loss their rigidity, poets began writing with rhyme and less attention to meter. However, all the Arabic poems translated in this compilation have a rhyme and meter but the rigidity of the meter is lessened in the more modern poems.

Marsin Alshamary

Plea to my Mother by Pier Paolo-Pasolini

"Supplica a miamadre" (Plea to my mother) was written by revered Italian intellectual, art critic, and poet Pier Paolo-Pasolini between 1961 and 1964, this poem is a son's plea for his mother to understand his homosexuality. At a time when Italy's social politics were (and still are) very closed to anything but heterosexuality, this poem expresses the anguish and tension Pasolini feels for what his mother's reaction might be, as well as the overwhelming love and connection that exists between Pasolini and his mother. The poem was also used in the film *Cento Passi* that featured Luigi lo Cascio as PeppinoImpastato, an 18 year old son of a Sicilian mafia boss who was ruthlessly abducted and killed by the mafia for a leftist anti-mafia radio show broadcasted around Sicily in the 70s. PeppinoImpastato was also gay, and the performance of this poem to his mother in the film is a graceful and touching allusion to the ideological and moral oppositions for which he fought.

Ali Rucker

الفداء

ابراهيم طوقان

لاتَسَـــل عَـن سَلامَته رُوحُهُ فَـوقَ راحَتِـه

بَـدَّلتـهُ هُمُـومُـه كَفَنـاً مِـن وسادَتِه

يَرقُـبُ السَّـــاعَةَ التى بَعـدَها هَـولُ ساعَتِه

شاغِلٌ فِكرُ مَن يَرا......ه بإطـراقٍ هـامَتِـه

بَيـنَ جَنبِـــهِ خافِقٌ يَتَلَظَّـى يغـايَتِـه

مَن رَأى فَحمَةَ الدُّجى أضرمَت مِن شَـرارتِـه

حَمَّـلتـهُ جَهَـنَّـــمٌ طَـرَفا مِـن رسالتِه

هُـوَ يالبـابِ واقِـــفٌ وَ الـرَّدى مِنـهُ خـائِف

قَاهدَأى يا عَواصِـفُ خَجَـلاً مِن جَراءَتِـه

صـامِتٌ لَو تَكَلَّـــما لَفَـظَ النَّـارَ وَ الـدَّمـا

قُل لِمَن عابَ صَمتَه خُـلِقَ الحَـزمُ أبكَـما

وَ أخُـو الحَزمِ لَم تَزل يَده تَسبِـقُ الفَـما

لاتَلـــوموه، قَـد رَأى مَنـهَجَ الحَـقٌ مُظلِـما

وَ يِـلاداً أحَبَّـــها رُكنُـها قَـد تَهَـدَّمَـا

وَ خُصُـوماً يَبغيـهِم ضَجَّتِ الارضُ وَ السَّما

... مَرَّ حينٌ، فَكـادَ يقتـله اليـأسُ، إنَّمـا

هُـوَ يالبـابِ واقِـفٌ وَ الرَّدى مِنـهُ خـائِف

قَاهـدَأى يا عَواصِفُ خَجـلاً مِـن جَراءَتِـه

1

The Patriot
By Ibrahim Touqan
Translated by Marsin Alshamary

Do not ask after him
For his soul is ready on his palm
Awaiting the hour that follows the last hour of his life
His bowed forehead worries all who see him
His heart rests between his sides, beating with a purpose
Whoever saw the blazes of first light darken from his passion
Hell makes him hold an edge of his message
He is standing in the doorway
And death fears him
O Storms! Be calm with reverence to his valor
Silent although he speaks
Utterances of fire and blood
Tell those who mock his silence
That determination was born a mute
And he, the brother of determination
His hand always precedes his tongue
Do not blame him, for he has seen
The pillars of justice wronged
And a country that he loved
Its pillars demolished
And enemies he detested
With the force of earth and heavens
Giddy, he was almost overtaken by grief, but
He is standing at the doorway
And death fears him
O Storms! Be calm with reverence to his valor

إرادة الحياة
أبو القاسم الشابي

فَلا بُدَّ أنْ يَسْتَجِيبَ القَدَر	إذا الشّعْبُ يَوْمَاً أرَادَ الحَيَاة
وَلا بُدَّ لِلقيْدِ أنْ يَنْكَسِر	وَلا بُدَّ لِلّيْل أنْ يَنْجَلِـي
تَبَخَّرَ في جَوِّهَا وَانْدَثَر	وَمَنْ لَمْ يُعَانِقْهُ شَوْقُ الحَيَاةِ
مِنْ صَفْعَةِ العَدَمِ المُنْتَصِر	فَوَيْلٌ لِمَنْ لَمْ تَشُقْهُ الحَيَاةُ
وَحَدّثَتْني رُوحُها المُسْتَتِر	كَذلِكَ قالتْ لِيَ الكائِنَاتُ
وَفَوْقَ الجِبَال وَتَحْتَ الشّجَر	وَدَمْدَمَتِ الرِّيحُ بَيْنَ الفِجَاج
رَكِبْتُ المُنَى وَنَسِيتُ الحَذَر	إذَا مَا طَمَحْتُ إلى غَـايَةٍ
وَلا كُبّة اللّهَبِ المُسْتَعِر	وَلَمْ أتَجَنّبْ وُعُورَ الشِّعَاب
يَعِشْ أبَدَ الدّهْرِ بَيْنَ الحُفَر	وَمَنْ لا يُحِبّ صُعُودَ الجِبَـالِ
وَضَجّتْ بصَدْري رِياحٌ أُخَر	فَعَجّتْ بِقلْبِي دِمَاءُ الشّبَابِ

3

The Desire for Life
By Abou-Alqasim Alshaby
Translated by Marsin Alshamary

If the people one day desire life

Then it cannot be but that fate responds

It cannot be but that night gives way

It cannot be but that bonds are broken

And he who is not embraced by life's longing

evaporates in its air and perishes

Cursed be he whom life has not weighed down

when want strikes him victoriously

The drumming of the winds between wide open roads

above the mountains and beneath the trees

If I do not strive towards a goal

and ride aspiration and forget caution

I did not avoid the winding paths in mountains

nor the burst of flames that I fell into

And he who cannot climb mountains

will live eternally between pits

The blood of the youth storms in my heart

وَعَزْفِ الرِّيَاح وَوَقعِ المَطَر
وَأَطْرَقتُ ، أُصْغِي لِقصْفِ الرُّعُودِ

" أيَا أُمُّ هَلْ تَكْرَهِينَ البَشَر؟"
وَقَالتْ لِيَ الأرْضُ ـ لَمَّا سَأَلتُ :

وَمَنْ يَسْتَلِذُّ رُكُوبَ الخَطَر
"أَبَاركُ في النَّاس أَهْلَ الطُّمُوح

وَيَقْنَعُ بالعَيْش عَيْش الحَجَر
وَألعَنُ مَنْ لا يُمَاشِي الزَّمَانَ

وَيَحْتَقِرُ المَيْتَ مَهْمَا كَبُر
هُوَ الكَوْنُ حَيٌّ ، يُحِبُّ الحَيَاة

وَلا النَّحْلُ يَلْثِمُ مَيْتَ الزَّهَـر
فَلا الأُفْقُ يَحْضُنُ مَيْتَ الطُّيُور

لَمَا ضَمَّتِ المَيْتَ تِلْكَ الحُفَر
وَلَـوْلا أُمومَةُ قلْبِي الرَّؤُوم

مِنْ لَعْنَةِ العَدَمِ المُنْتَصِر!"
فَوَيْلٌ لِمَنْ لَمْ تَشُقْهُ الحَيَاةُ

مُثَقَّلَةٍ بالأسَى وَالضَّجَر
وفي لَيْلَةٍ مِنْ لَيَالِي الخَرِيفِ

And other winds roar in my chest

I bowed my head, listening to the thunder's bombing

the symphony of winds, the falling rain

And the earth told me-when I asked

"O, Mother, do you hate humanity?"

"I bless the ambitious amongst people

and those who enjoy riding danger

And I curse those who do not hurry time

who are satisfied with living the life of stone

The universe is living, loving life

and hating the dead, no matter how grand

The horizon does not embrace dead birds

nor do bees kiss dead blossoms

And if not for my maternal heart, then

I would not have enclosed the dead in holes

Cursed be he who life hasn't weighed down

when want strikes him victoriously!"

And in one night amongst the nights of autumn

laden with sorrow and tedium

سَكِرْتُ بِهَا مِنْ ضِيَاءِ النُّجُومِ   وَغَنَّيْتُ لِلْحُزْنِ حَتَّى سَكِر

سَأَلْتُ الدُّجَى: هَلْ تُعِيدُ الحَيَاةُ   لِمَا أَذْبَلَتْهُ رَبِيعَ العُمُرِ؟

فَلَمْ تَتَكَلَّمْ شِفَاهُ الظَّلامِ   وَلَمْ تَتَرَنَّمْ عَذَارَى السَّحَر

وَقَالَ لِيَ الغَابُ فِي رِقَّةٍ   مُحَبَّبَةٍ مِثْلَ خَفْقِ الوَتَر

يَجِيءُ الشِّتَاءُ ، شِتَاءُ الضَّبَابِ   شِتَاءُ الثُّلُوجِ ، شِتَاءُ المَطَر

فَيَنْطَفِىءُ السِّحْرُ ، سِحْرُ الغُصُونِ   وَسِحْرُ الزُّهُورِ وَسِحْرُ الثَّمَر

وَسِحْرُ المَسَاءِ الشَّجِيِّ الوَدِيعِ   وَسِحْرُ المُرُوجِ الشَّهِيِّ العَطِر

وَتَهْوِي الغُصُونُ وَأَوْرَاقُهَا   وَأَزْهَارُ عَهْدٍ حَبِيبٍ نَضِر

وَتَلْهُو بِهَا الرِّيحُ فِي كُلِّ وَادٍ   وَيَدْفِنُهَا السَّيْلُ أَنَّى عَبَر

وَيَفْنَى الجَمِيعُ كَحُلْمٍ بَدِيعِ   تَأَلَّقَ فِي مُهْجَةٍ وَانْدَثَر

Drunken from the starlight

I sang to sadness till it was drunk

I asked the deepest night: "will life return

to those whose life's spring has withered?"

The lips of the darkness did not speak

nor did the early light chant

And the forest told me delicately

lovely as quivering violin strings

Winter will come, winter of fog

winter of snow, winter of rain

The charm will flicker, the charm of vines

the charm of flowers, the charm of harvest

The melancholy charm of the evening

the charm of waves delicious and fragrant

The branches and their leaves sway

and the flowers of a glowing time

The winds will sway them in every valley

and the torrents will bury them

And everything will be ended

like the end of a happy dream

وَتَبْقَى البُدُورُ التي حُمِّلَتْ   ذَخِيرَةَ عُمْرٍ جَمِيلٍ غَبَر
وَذِكْرَى فُصُولٍ ، وَرُؤْيَا حَيَاةٍ   وَأَشْبَاح دُنْيَا تَلاشَتْ زُمَر
مُعَانِقَة وَهْيَ تَحْتَ الضَّبَابِ   وَتَحْتَ الثُّلُوج وَتَحْتَ المَدَر
لَطِيفَ الحَيَاةِ الذي لا يُمَلُّ   وَقَلبَ الرَّبيع الشَّذِيِّ الخَضِر
وَحَالِمَة بأَغَانِي الطُّيُور   وَعِطْرِ الزُّهُور وَطَعْم الثَّمَر

"ويَمشِي الزَّمانُ، فتنموْ صُروفٌ   وتذْوي صُروفٌ، وتحْيا أخَر
وتُصبح أحلامُها يَقْظة،   مُوَشَّحة بغُموض السَّحر
تُسائِلُ: أينَ ضَبابُ الصَّباح،   وَسِحْرُ المساء؟ وضوْءُ القَمر؟
وَأسرابُ ذاكَ الفَراش الأنِيق؟   ونَحْلٌ يُغَنِي، وغَيْمٌ يَمُرّ
وأينَ الأشِعَّةُ والكائِناتُ؟   وأينَ الحياةُ التّي أنْتَظِر

9

The seeds will remain, laden

that were hoarded by a beautiful completed life

The memory of seasons, the vision of life

and ghosts of a world that dissipated

Embracing, while under the fog

under the snow, under the dried clay

The best of life, that which does not bore

the heart of spring, fragrant and verdant

Dreaming of the songs of birds

the perfume of flowers, the taste of fruits

Time passes and occasions are cultivated

occasions wither and others come to life

And her dreams become a reality

Swathed in the darkness of early light

She asks: "where is the morning fog?

The charm of the evening? The moonlight?

that flock of elegant birds

And the bees murmuring, and storm clouds passing

And where is the radiating light and the creatures?

And where is the life I am waiting for?

ظمِئتُ إلى النُّور، فوقَ العُصون!	ظمِئتُ إلى الظِّلِّ تحتَ الشَّجار!

ظمِئتُ إلى النَّبْعِ، بَيْنَ المُروج	يُغَنِّين ويّرْقُصُ فوْقَ الزّهَرَ!

ظمِئتُ إلى نَغَمَتِ الطُّيور،	وهَمس النَّسيم، ولحْن المَطر!

ظمِئتُ إلى الكون! أيْنَ الوُجودُ	وأنّي أرَى العالمَ المنتظر

هو الكَوْنُ، خَلَفَ سُباتِ الجُمود	وفي أثْقُق اليَقَظاتِ الكُبَر"

ومَا هُوَ إلاّ كَخَفْق الجَنَاح	حَتَّى نَمَا شَوْقُهَا وانْتَصَر

فصَدّعت الأرض من فوقها	وأبصرت الكون عذب الصور

وجاءَ الربيعُ بأنغامـه	وأحلامـهِ وصِبـاهُ العطِر

وقبّلـها قبـلاً في الشفاه	تعيد الشباب الذي قد غبر

وخُلْدتِ في نسلكِ المُدّخر	وقالَ لهَا : قد مُنحتِ الحياةَ

11

I thirsted for light above the branches!

I thirsted for the shade under the trees!

I thirsted for the spring between the waves

Dancing and singing above the flowers

I thirsted for the birds' melody!

And the whisper of breezes, the symphony of rain!

I thirsted for the universe! Where is existence?

 I see the awaited world

It is the universe, before a frozen hibernation

In the deepest awakenings

It is nothing but the beating of wings

until its excitement heightens and is completed

Then the earth split and rose up

presenting the universe with the most vibrant vision

The spring then came

with his tunes, his dreams, and his fragrant youth

And he kissed her, a kiss on the lips

a kiss that returned the youth that faded

And told her "you have been granted life

and been immortalized in your hoarded seeds

وباركِكِ النورُ فاستقبلي   شبابَ الحياةِ وخصبَ العُمر
ومن تعبدُ النورَ أحلامُهُ   يباركهُ النورُ أنّى ظهر
إليك الفضاء ، إليك الضياء   إليك الثرى الحالِمِ المُزْدَهِر
إليك الجمال الذي لا يبيد   إليك الوجود الرحيب النضر
فميدي كما شئتِ فوق الحقول   بحلو الثمار وغض الزهر
وناجي النسيم وناجي الغيوم   وناجي النجوم وناجي القمـر
وناجي الحيـاة وأشواقها   وفتنـة هذا الوجود الأغـر

وشف الدجى عن جمال عميقٍ   يشب الخيـال ويذكي الفكر
ومُدَّ عَلَى الكَوْن سِحْرٌ غَريبٌ   يُصَرِّفُهُ سَاحِرٌ مُقْتَدِر

13

The light has blessed you

so welcome youth and the ripe age

And he whose dreams worship the light

the light will bless him whenever he appears

To you space, to you light

to you the blossoming soil

To you beauty that does not fade

to you the glowing existence

So frisk as you wish above the fields

bejeweled in beautiful fruits and verdant blossoms

And mingle amongst the breezes

the stars, and the moon

React with life and its desires

and the beauty of this existence

The deepest night began to end

with a strange beauty

That refreshes the imagination

and nurtures inspiration

A strange magic is spread across the universe

by the hands of a capable sorcerer

وَضَاعَ البَخُورُ ، بَخُورُ الزَّهَر   وَضَاءَتْ شُمُوعُ النُّجُومِ الوِضَاء

بِأَجْنِحَةٍ مِنْ ضِيَاءِ القَمَر   وَرَفْرَفَ رُوحٌ غَرِيبُ الجَمَال

في هَيْكَلٍ حَالِمٍ قَدْ سُحِر   وَرَنَّ نَشِيدُ الحَيَاةِ المُقَدَّس

لَهِيبُ الحَيَاةِ وَرُوحُ الظَّفَر   وَأَعْلَنَ في الكَوْنِ أَنَّ الطُّمُوحَ

فلا بُدَّ أَنْ يَسْتَجِيبَ القَدَرْ   إِذا طَمَحَتْ لِلحَيَاةِ النُّفُوس

15

The lamps of the stars are lit

and the incense of flowers

A soul flickered, of strange beauty

with wings of moonlight

The sacred chant of life rang

in an imagined structure

Announcing to the universe

that ambition is the flame of life, the soul of victory

If souls aspire to life

it cannot be but that fate responds

مالي وقفت على القبور مسلما   قبر الحبيب فلم يرد جوابى

احبيب: ما لك لا ترد جوابنا   انسيت بعدي خلة الاحباب؟

قال الحبيب: و كيف لي بجوابكم   و انا رهين جنادل و تراب!

اكل التراب محاسني فنسيتكم   و حجبت عن اهلي و عن اترابي

فعليكم منّي السّلام تقطّعت   منّي و منكم خلة الاحباب

علي بن ابي طالب رضي الله عنه

May Allah be Satisfied by Ali Ibn Abi Talib

Translated by Rayhan El-Alami

What is wrong that I stand at the graveside greeting the grave
of the Beloved, yet he
Does not return my greeting?
Oh Beloved, why do you not return my greeting?
Have you forgotten the closeness between those who love?
'How can I reply?' The Beloved speaks,
'When I am a prisoner of shattered stone and dusty soil?
The earth has consumed my lovely features,
and I am hid from my kin and my companions,
Such is my greeting to you, for lost to me and to you is the
closeness
Between those who love.'

吾尝终日而思矣，不如须臾之所学也。吾尝跂而望矣，不如登高之博**见**也。登高而招，臂非加**长**也，而**见**者远；顺**风**而呼，声非加疾也，而闻者彰。假舆**马**者，非利足也，而致千里；假舟楫者，非能水也，而绝江河。君子生非异也，善假于物也。

The Art of Learning by Xunzi

Translated by Yue Xing

I used to think and brood every day, but I could not acquire as much as what I could have learnt within a limited time. I used to try to look farther by standing on my toe, but I could not see as broad as when I was on a hill. If you wave when you are at a higher place, though your arms do not grow longer, others can still see you from a distance. If you call someone along the distance of the wind, though you do not tune up your voice, others can hear you more clearly. As people make use of carriages and horses, they can cover more distance than others without being fast walkers. As people take advantage of boats and ships, they can go across the river without being able to swim. People are not born differently by nature, but it is the ability to discover aiding facilities that make a person distinguished from others.

别愁 （一剪梅）

李清照

红藕香残玉簟秋。轻解罗裳，独上兰舟。

云中谁寄锦书来，雁字回时，月满西楼。

花自飘零水自流。一种相思，两处闲愁。

此情无计可消除，才下眉头，却上心头。

The Sorrow of Separation by Li Qingzhao

Translated by Wendy Chen

Li Qingzhao (1084—c.1151) is one of the few eminent women
poets in China. She wrote this poem while separated from her
husband, who was off fighting in war.
(Sung to the Melody of "A Sprig of Plum Blossoms")

With autumn comes the fading fragrance of wilting red lotuses
and the cooling of the bamboo mats.
I lift my long silk skirt to step
into a small riverboat, alone.
Who from the white clouds will bring me a brocade letter?[1]
I will wait even until the migrating swan-geese return
and the moonlight illuminates my house in the west.

As the flowers drift and the water runs down,
we share one longing for each other
though separated by distance.
This sorrow is unrelenting,
an ache flowing from my head
to my heart.

---

[1] Alluding to a traditional fairytale in which two lovers send their
letters, made of Chinese characters embroidered on brocade cloth, by
swan-geese that migrate back and forth across the country.

"Le mur ou les charmes d'une vie conjugale" de Myriam Warner-Vieyra

Mariée depuis plusieurs années avec un homme sage, fidèle, sérieux, calme - le rêve de beaucoup de femmes qui se plaignent de leur macho infidèle, volage, menteur ou jaloux -, je vais vous croquer vingt-quatre heures de ma vie auprès de cet être merveilleux.

Un soir vers vingt et une heures trente, il me dit :
- Passe-moi la clé de ta voiture.
- Oui. Il faudra mettre de l'essence, le réservoir a juste la quantité nécessaire pour mes courses de la semaine.

Il m'avait parlé ! La dernière fois que nous avions échangé trois mots remontait à je ne sais plus combien de temps : plusieurs jours, une ou deux semaines...Incroyable ! Ma réponse avait fusé spontanément pour dire quelque chose, établir un dialogue. Balivernes insipides : l'essence, cela n'avait aucune importance.

Comment en étions-nous arrivés là ? En toute sincérité, je ne le savais pas. Où se situait ma part de responsabilité ? Dans le passé je m'appliquais à meubler les silences, je parlais beaucoup. De temps en temps, un grognement que je prenais pour un encouragement me remontait comme une vieille pendule. Je plaisantais, riais de mes trouvailles, espérant que mon rire le contaminerait. Son aphasie épouvantait mes amis qui disparurent l'un après l'autre de notre foyer réfrigérant. Puis je fus lasse de m'entendre répondre à mes propres questions. Désespérée de ne pas réussir à faire naître un sourire ou un mot aimable sur les lèvres de mon époux, je me suis bétonnée dans le mutisme, moi aussi.

Ma voisine de palier me regarde avec envie et admiration. Chaque fin de semaine, son mari rentre ivre vers quatre heures du matin et fait un vacarme à fendre la tête d'un sourd en martelant leur porte d'entrée de coups de pieds ; tandis que dans notre appartement, trois cent soixante-cinq jours par an plane un silence de cimetière.

"The Wall or The Charms of a Married Life" by Myriam Warner-Vieyra from *Femmes échouées : nouvelles* (Paris : Présence Africaine, 1988)

Translated by Eleanor A. Fulvio

Married for several years to a wise, loyal, serious, calm man - the dream of many women who complain about their macho, unfaithful, fickle, lying or jealous men - I am going to sketch a picture for you of twenty-four hours of my life with this marvelous being.

One night around 9:30, he says to me, "Pass me the keys to your car."

"Okay. It needs gas. The tank has just enough for my shopping for the week."

He had spoken to me! The last time that we had exchanged even three words goes back to I no longer know when--several days, one or two weeks ago...Incredible! My response had burst out spontaneously so as to say *something*, establish a dialogue. Insipid nonsense: gasoline, of no consequence.

How had we gotten there? In all sincerity, I didn't know. Where was my part of the responsibility? In the past, I would take it upon myself to fill the silences; I would talk a lot. From time to time, a grunt which I took as encouragement would come back to me like the hollow sound of an old pendulum. I would make jokes and laugh at them myself, hoping that my levity would be catching. His aphasia disconcerted my friends who disappeared one after the other from our austere dwelling. Then, I wearied of hearing myself answer my own questions. Despairing of ever succeeding in sparking a smile or a kind word from the lips of my spouse, I, too, closed myself off in silence.

My neighbor looks at me with envy and admiration. Each weekend, her husband returns drunk around 4:00 in the morning and makes such a racket that it would give even a deaf man a headache, hammering their door with his feet; whereas, in our apartment, 365 days a year hangs the silence of a cemetery.

A vingt-deux heures, douchée, cheveux brossés, dents curées, je me glisse entre les draps du lit comme une lettre dans une enveloppe toute neuve. Draps de chez un grand couturier en vogue ; malgré la griffe bien visible, il ne s'en est jamais aperçu. C'aurait pu être deux vieux pagnes, deux sacs à farine, pour lui c'était du pareil au même. Il y a bien longtemps, pour notre mariage, une amie m'offrit une paire de draps en satin or. Un soir, je revêtis une chemise de nuit assortie et défis largement le lit, sûre d'être irrésistible ainsi parée. C'était au temps où il parlait quelquefois. Alors il éructa :

- Qu'est-ce que c'est que ce truc-là ?

Question qui me rendit muette d'indignation.

Ce soir, monsieur n'ayant pas dit où il allait ni quand il rentrerait, j'étains ma lampe de chevet et m'endors sur mes points d'interrogation. Le lendemain matin, à sept heures, je me lève. "Le Mur", comme je l'appelle désormais, dort. Je ne sais pas à quelle heure il est rentré. C'est sans importance ! Quelle différence entre un mur présent et un mur absent ? A bien réfléchir, il y en a une : sa présence immobile et silencieuse m'énerve, j'ai envie de le détruire à coups de marteau. En son absence, je me sens calme, mais vide de toute énergie, désoeuvrée.

Sept heures trente. Je quitte la maison, rentre dans le monde ; enfin du bruit, des paroles. Je m'arrête à la pâtisserie, toujours la même à la même heure. J'achète mes croissants quotidiens, salue les habitués vissés à leur table, dégustant un café moins bon que celui préparé chez eux, cependant tellement plus agréable en compagnie des copains, tout en commentant les dernières nouvelles.

Arrivée au bureau, sevrée d'échanges d'idées depuis plus de douze heures, je forme un numéro sur le cadran du téléphone avant d'entamer ma tâche du jour. Enfin à l'autre bout une voix amie ; je peux parler et elle me répond, souvent très aimable. Aujourd'hui malheureusement je sens de l'agacement, une certaine froideur, de l'impatience, des silences qui en disent long. C'est que je dérange. Je prie que l'on veuille bien m'excuser et raccroche.

At 10:00 p.m., showered, hair brushed, teeth cleaned, I slip between the sheets of the bed like a letter into an envelope. Sheets from a stylish big-name designer; despite the obvious label, he has never noticed it. It could have been two old loincloths, two flour sacks--for him, it was all the same. Quite some time ago, for our marriage, a friend gave me a pair of sheets in gold satin. One night, I put on a matching chemise and spread out across the bed, sure to be irresistible thus arrayed. This was at the time when he used to speak occasionally. He spit out, "What is *that* thing?"

His question left me speechless with indignation.

Tonight, since monsieur had not said where he was going or when he would return, I turn off the bedside lamp and go to sleep on my uncertainties. The next morning at 7:00, I get up. "The Wall", as I will call him from now on, is sleeping. I don't know what time he came back. No big deal! What difference is there between a wall that is present and a wall that is absent? Now that I think about it, there is one: its immobile and silent presence puts me on edge; I'd like to destroy it with a hammer. In its absence, I feel calm, but empty of all energy, idle.

7:30 a.m. I leave the house, go back out into the world-- finally some noise, some words. I stop by the patisserie, always the same thing at the same time. I buy my daily croissants and greet the regulars glued to their chairs, sipping coffee that's not as good as what they could have prepared at home yet so much more pleasant when taken in the company of friends and, all the while, commenting on the latest news.

Having arrived at the office, deprived of the exchange of ideas for over twelve hours, I dial a number on the telephone before starting my first task of the day. Finally, on the other end, a friendly voice; I can speak and she responds to me, often very amiably. Unfortunately, today I sense irritation, a certain impatient coldness. I'm disturbing her. I apologize for the annoyance and hang up.

Cette petite goutte d'indifférence fait déborder mon coeur de son trop-plein d'angoisse. Malgré moi, je me mets bêtement à pleurer. Je me sens désespérément seule dans un monde hostile. Personne ne veut m'écouter, me parler. Je suis entourée d'égocentriques bienheureux. Leur dire : "Aujourd'hui j'ai le cafard, parlez-moi, j'ai besoin d'être rassurée". Ils s'en moquent. "Allez vous faire pendre ailleurs ! Surtout pas sous nos yeux. Laissez-nous notre sérénité, gardez vos tracas." Les heures s'étirent avec une lenteur cruelle, en milliers de secondes vides d'espoir.

A douze heures trente, de retour à la maison, le Mur n'est pas encore là ; je l'attends, feuilletant une revue pour écourter le temps. Il arrive vingt minutes plus tard, utilise sa clé pour rentrer, va directement dans la salle de bains puis vient s'installer à table avec son poste à transistor ; il ne rate jamais les informations. Ce qui se passe dans le monde l'intéresse, il lit tous les journaux de toutes opinions pour mieux se faire la sienne. Depuis le jour où j'ai hurlé que j'en avais plein le gosier des atrocités que débite l'actualité, il s'est acheté un casque à écouteurs. Je n'entends que les cliquetis des fourchettes et couteaux sur les assiettes. Au dessert, l'acidité de l'orange qu'il mange lui fait grincer les dents et me tourne le sang. Je suis à deux doigts de la crise de nerfs. Il se retire dans la chambre pour faire sa sieste, j'allume une cigarette ; je ne risque pas de mourir d'un cancer du poumon ou de la gorge, bien avant mon cerveau va éclater de toute la rage contenue dans cet étau qui me comprime les tempes et le front.

A quatorze heures trente, je repars, retrouve mon bureau. Les murs sont lézardés, la peinture écaillée, le patron absent, les clients rares. A qui pourrais-je bien téléphoner ? Le je-m'en-foutisme de la voix amie, ce matin, m'a déçue. Mes copines on l'air tout épanouies, heureuses. Elles sont toujours occupées, pressées, entre un rendez-vous chez le coiffeur, la couturière, le thé bridge, leur emploi, leur mari, leurs enfants. Je suis tout étourdie de les voir si affairées.

J'essaie de travailler, mon esprit vagabonde. Je décroche le téléphone, j'hésite entre deux bonnes amies. J'appelle :

This little bit of indifference overwhelms me with excessive anguish. In spite of myself, I start stupidly to cry. I feel desperately alone in a hostile world. No one wants to listen to me or speak to me. I'm surrounded by blissful egocentrics. Say to them, "I'm feeling down today. Speak to me. I need to be reassured." They couldn't care less. "Go tell your problems to someone else! Leave us alone. Keep your worries to yourself." The hours stretch out cruelly, millions of seconds empty of hope.

At 12:30 p.m., I'm home and the Wall isn't there yet; I wait for him, leafing through a magazine to kill time. He arrives twenty minutes later, uses his key to open the door, goes directly to the bathroom, then comes to sit down at the table with his radio; he never misses the news. What goes on in the world interests him; he reads all the newspapers of differing opinions in order to better form his own. Since the day I yelled that I had had it up to here with the atrocities in the news, he bought himself headphones. I hear only the clinking of forks and knives on the plates. During dessert, the acidity of the orange he's eating makes him grind his teeth which turns my stomach. I am very near hysterics. He retires to his room for a nap. I light a cigarette; my brain will explode from all the rage contained in this grip which squeezes my temples and forehead before I ever run the risk of dying of lung or throat cancer.

At 2:30 p.m., I leave again to go back to the office. The walls are cracked, the paint chipped, the boss is absent, the clients are few and far between. Who could I phone? The apathetic attitude of my friend this morning disheartened me. My friends seem fulfilled and happy. They are always busy, in a rush, between appointments with the hairdresser, the dressmaker, a tea, their work, their husbands, their children. I am dazed to think of them so preoccupied.

I try to work, my mind wandering. I pick up the phone and hesitate, deciding between two good friends. I call:

l'une n'est pas dans son bureau ; l'autre, qui ne travaille pas, vient de sortir. Je repose doucement le combiné, mon regard caresse avec volupté sa ligne racée dans sa robe couleur de brume matinale. Je me surprends à souhaiter très fort qu'il sonne. A la minute qui sait, mon voeu est exaucé. Les battements de mon coeur se précipitent, enfin quelqu'un pense à moi. Je respire profondément, racle ma gorge pour éclaircir ma voix, décroche, et avec beaucoup d'assurance, lance comme un cocorico un " allo ! " joyeux.

- Bonjour. Je voudrais parler au capitaine.

- Comment ?

- C'est bien la caserne des pompiers ?

Je serre les lèvres pour ne pas lâcher une insanité. Mon interlocuteur n'est pour rien dans ma déconvenue. Au bout de quelques secondes je parviens à gargouiller un "non" mouillé d'ennui.

L'après-midi tire tout de même à sa fin. Je fais quelques achats sur le chemin du retour, et à dix-neuf heures, je retrouve le Mur, déjà en pyjama, pantoufles aux pieds, son verre de whisky servi. Lèvres entrouvertes, sourire béat, il gobe un match de football à la télévision, il n'a pas un regard de mon côté. Vers vingt heures, nous dégustons notre souper dans un silence velouté. Le vent murmure dans les branches des arbres de la cour de l'immeuble, accompagnant notre duo où les notes sont figurées par les soupirs, les demi-soupirs, les pauses, les demi-pauses, altérés de points d'orgue. Je suis relativement paisible. L'habitude.

Il se met au lit et plonge dans la lecture de ses nombreux journaux. A vingt et une heures trente, je le rejoins dans notre chambre. Le ventilateur brasse avec peine l'air emmuré. Le réveil-matin à quartz rougeoie sans bruit. Je prends un livre : *Madame Bovary*. Elle avait un mari qui l'adorait, lui parlait, elle n'était pas heureuse pourtant. Qu'aurait-elle fait à ma place ? Je serais curieuse de savoir s'il existe une femme capable d'envier ma solitude givrée. Les petites misères de madame Bovary ne me distraient pas, ne me consolent pas. J'ai besoin de parler,

one is not at her desk; the other, who doesn't work, has just gone out. I gently put down the receiver, my gaze voluptuously caressing it's elegant lines the color of morning mist. I surprise myself by my yearning for it to ring. At that moment, my wish is granted. My heart races, at last someone is thinking about me. I take a deep breath, clear my throat, pick up the receiver, and confidently exclaim a joyous "Hello!" as though crowing a cock-a-doodle-do.

"Hello. I would like to speak to the captain."

"I'm sorry?"

"This *is* the fire station, right?"

I bite my tongue to avoid blurting out anything rude. The person I'm talking to is an unwitting participant in my disappointment. After several seconds, I manage to gurgle a melancholy "no".

The afternoon draws to a close all the same. I make some purchases on the way home, and at 7:00 p.m., I discover the Wall already in pajamas, slippers on his feet, his glass of whisky poured. Lips parted in a rapturous smile, immersed in a soccer game on TV, he doesn't even cast a glance at me. Around 8:00 p.m., we eat our supper in a mellow silence. The breeze murmurs in the tree branches in the courtyard of the apartment building, accompanying our duet of quarter rests, eighth rests, rests, half rests, broken up by fermatas. I am relatively peaceful. The routine.

He goes to bed and dives into reading his numerous newspapers. At 9:30 p.m., I join him in our room. The fan blows the trapped air around with difficulty. The quartz alarm clock glows red noiselessly. I take a book: *Madame Bovary*. She had a husband who adored her, spoke to her; yet she wasn't happy. What would she have done in my place? I would be curious to know if there exists a woman capable of envying my icy solitude. The little troubles of Madame Bovary don't distract me, don't console me. I need to speak,

de parler à quelqu'un qui m'écouterait, qui répondrait à mes questions. Entendre le son d'une voix, des mots aimables, des compliments, des mots caressants, des flatteries et même des mensonges qui comblent de joie en attendant l'heure de vérité, qui peut d'ailleurs ne jamais venir troubler une innocente quiétude.

Je vois le Mur de profil, il dévore des yeux son journal. L'unique son que l'on perçoive, c'est le léger bruissement des feuilles qu'il tourne de temps en temps. Je sens gronder en moi une sourde révolte. Cela ne peut pas continuer ! Je peux partir, bien sûr, qui m'en empêche ? Mais après tant d'années de silence, ne suis-je pas devenue moi aussi un être singulier ? Pourrais-je m'habituer à une autre vie ? Loin du Mur ? Partir, c'est peut-être transporter sous d'autres cieux mon ennui. Je suis maintenant trop lasse, le chemin parcouru trop long. On ne peut pas indéfiniment revenir en arrière et raccommoder le passé comme une vieille blouse déchirée. Trop tard. Si je me tuais ? Quelle blague ! Ha ! ha ! ha ! Je ne serais même pas là pour voir si le Mur verserait une larme. D'ailleurs il ne comprendrait pas. Personne d'autre non plus. Partir ! Mourir ! Partir ! Mourir ! Partir...Mourir...Et si je me jetais sur lui en le frappant ? Il finirait pas ouvrir la bouche enfin...J'en ai marre...Marre à bout...Bout de ficelle...

Merde ! Merde ! Merde ! C'est assez. Plus de sagesse, de bon sens, de conformisme, je veux du bruit. J'éclate de rire. Dépassée par ma propre excitation je rejette les draps, arrache ma chemise de nuit, saute sur le lit en criant, gesticulant. Je veux extirper cet homme de sa tranquillité qui m'enrage, faire écrouler ce mur d'indifférence. Je tombe sur lui, relève la tête.

Il me regarde, étonné, rajuste ses lunettes puis reprend sa lecture. Sans un mot.

to speak to someone who would listen to me, who would respond to my questions. To hear the sound of a voice, of friendly words, of compliments, of affectionate words, of flatteries and even of lies that fill one with joy while awaiting the hour of truth, for that matter, of lies that can never really trouble an innocent tranquillity.

I see the profile of the Wall, devouring his newspaper with his eyes. The only perceptible sound is the light rustling of the pages as he turns them from time to time. I feel a faint revolt brewing inside of me. This cannot continue! I could certainly leave. Who would stop me? But after so many years of silence, haven't I also become a detached being? Could I get used to another life? Far from the Wall? Leaving might simply mean transferring my same old ennui to a new setting. I am too weary now, have traveled too far. We cannot go back indefinitely to mend the past as we would an old, torn blouse. Too late. If I killed myself? What a joke! Ha! ha! ha! I wouldn't even be there to see if the Wall would shed a tear. Anyway, he wouldn't understand. Nor would anyone else. Leave! Die! Leave! Die! Leave...Die...And if I threw myself on him and hit him? He would end up finally opening his mouth...I'm sick of it...Sick to the core...At the end of my rope...

Shit! Shit! Shit! Enough. No more wisdom, common sense, conformism, I want noise. I crack up with laughter. Overcome by my own excitement, I throw back the covers, rend my nightgown, jump on the bed screaming and gesticulating. I want to drag this man out from his tranquil stupor that enrages me, to tear down this wall of indifference. I fall on him then raise my head.

He looks at me, surprised, readjusts his glasses then takes up his reading once more. Without a word.

Les Feuilles Mortes

Jacques Prévert

Oh ! Je voudrais tant que tu te souviennes
Des jours heureux où nous étions amis.
En ce temps-là la vie était plus belle,
Et le soleil plus brillant qu'aujourd'hui.
Les feuilles mortes se ramassent ?la pelle.
Tu vois, je n'ai pas oubli?
Les feuilles mortes se ramassent à la pelle,
Les souvenirs et les regrets aussi
Et le vent du nord les emporte
Dans la nuit froide de l'oubli.
Tu vois, je n'ai pas oubli?

La chanson que tu me chantais.

[Refrain:]
C'est une chanson qui nous ressemble.
Toi, tu m'aimais et je t'aimais
Et nous vivions tous deux ensembles,
Toi qui m'aimais, moi qui t'aimais.
Mais la vie sépare ceux qui s'aiment,
Tout doucement, sans faire de bruit
Et la mer efface sur le sable
Les pas des amants désunis.

Les feuilles mortes se ramassent ?la pelle,
Les souvenirs et les regrets aussi

Dead Leaves
By Jacques Prévert

Translated by Marianne Yakun Xu

Oh! I wish you could remember
The glorious days when we were still friends
Then, life was more beautiful,
And the sun brighter than today.
Dead leaves are piling up by the dozen
See, I haven't forgotten
Dead leaves are piling up by the dozen,
Like memories and regrets
That the northern wind carries
Into the cold night of oblivion
See, I haven't forgotten
The song you sang to me.

It is a song that resembles us
You, you loved me and I loved you
And we lived together, just the two of us
You who loved me, I who loved you
But Life pulls apart those who love each other
So gently without a noise
And the sea washes away from the sand
Footprints of fractured lovers.
Dead leaves are piling up by the dozen
Like memories and regrets

Mais mon amour silencieux et fidèle
Sourit toujours et remercie la vie.
Je t'aimais tant, tu étais si jolie.
Comment veux-tu que je t'oublie ?
En ce temps-l? La vie était plus belle
Et le soleil plus brillant qu'aujourd'hui.
Tu étais ma plus douce amie
Mais je n'ai que faire des regrets
Et la chanson que tu chantais,
Toujours, toujours je l'entendrai !

But my love, silent and loyal
Forever smiles and gives thanks to Life
I loved you so, you were so pretty,
How can you expect me to forget you?
Then, life was more beautiful
And the sun brighter than today
You were my sweetest friend
But now I can only regret
And the song that you sang to me
Forever, forever I will hear it!

La Remontée des cendres

Tahar Ben Jelloun

Ce corps qui fut un rire
brûle à présent.
Cendres emportées par le vent jusqu'au fleuve
et l'eau les reçoit comme les restes de larmes
  heureuses.
Cendres d'une mémoire où perle une petite vie
bien simple, une vie sans histoire, avec un jardin,
une fontaine et quelques livres.
Cendres d'un corps échappé à la fosse commune
offertes à la tempête des sables.

Quand le vent se lèvera, ces cendres iront se poser
  sur les yeux des vivants.
Ceux-ci n'en sauront rien
ils marcheront triomphants avec un peu de mort
  sur le visage.

Innombrables sont les signes se vidant de leur eau
dans le tumulte de l'extrême
là, au bord d'un cimetière mouvant.

The Rise of Ashes by Tahar Ben Jelloun

Translated by Glenna Moran

This body that was a laugh

now burns.

Ashes are wafted by the wind to the river

and the water receives them like the remains of

happy tears.

Ashes of a memory where a small, simple life forms,

a life without history, with a garden,

a fountain, and a few books.

Ashes of a body escaped from the collective grave

offered to the sandstorm.

When the wind rises, these ashes will settle

on the eyes of the living.

They will realize nothing

they will walk triumphant with a fragment of death

on their faces.

Countless are the signs emptying of their water

in the tumult of the boundary

there, at the edge of a moving cemetery.

ვაჟა—ფშაველა
სტუმარ-მასპინძელი

I
ღამის წყვდიადში ჩაფლული,
გამტკნარებულის სახითა,
მოსჩანს ქისტეთის მიდამო
სალის კლდეების ტახტითა.
ბნელს ხევზე მოჰყეფს მდინარე,
გულამღვრეული ჯავრითა.
გადმოხრილიყვნენ მთანიცა,
ხელ-პირს იბანდენ წყალზედა;
ზევრი მომკვდარა მათს მკერდზე,
სისხლს ვერ იხდენენ ტანზედა;
ძმის მკვლელის სისხლი სწყურია,
კაცი რამ მოდის გზაზედა.
გზას ვამბობ, თორემ რა გზაა.
ვიწრო ბილიკი კლდეზედა?
სავალად მეტად ძნელია,
ფეხს ძლივს აციელებს ფეხზედა.
გალმა სჩანს ქისტის სოფელი
არწივის ბუდესავითა, -
საამო არის საცქერლად
დიაცის უბესავითა.
სოფლის თავს სძინავს შავს ნისლსა
დაფიქრებულის სახითა.
ყურს უგდებს არე-მარესა,
გულ-ლაღობს სანახავითა.
სტუმარი ცოტა ხანისა
ხვალ სხვაგან წავა აქითა.
წავა, გადივლის გორებსა,

Host and Guest by Vazha-Pshavela
Translated by Lela Jgerenaia

I

Veiled in the gloom of night
The sweet face of Kisteti
Appears, among hills around,
A rocky throne among cliffs.
The river moans in its dark ravine
Turbid, with grief at its heart.
The mountains too are bowed down,
Laving face and hands in the water;
On their breasts, many have died,
Unfitting is the blood on their flanks.
Seeking the blood of his brother's killer,
A man travels along the road.
I say a road, but what road is this:
A narrow path over rock!
A path that's so hard to walk,
He can scarcely move a step.
There, the village of the Kists,
Is like an eagle's nest,
As pleasant a place to gaze on
As the breast of a woman.
Black fog slumbers about the village,
Its face deep in thought,
Listening to the hills around,
Absorbing the scene with joy.
It's a guest for the moment,
Tomorrow, it moves elsewhere;
Departing, travelling the heights,

40

ქედებსა ყინულიანსა;
აზნელებს, უხილავად ჰქმნის
ქვეყანას ხილულიანსა.
თუ მონადირეს აჩირებს,
გზა-დაკარგულსა კლდეშია,
ალაღებს მგელსა და ქურდსა,
მოარულთ სიბნელეშია.

II

ზევიდამ ვინღაც უცნობმა
კლდის ლოდი გადმოაგორა,
მგზავრმა შეჰხედა პირ-აღმე,
წინ უდგას მაღალი გორა.
ყურს უგდებს... ცოტა ხანს შემდეგ
მოესმა ქვიშის ჩხრიალი.
მგზავრი სიათას იმარჯვებს:
მტერი არ იყოს ტიალი.
შესცქერის გაფაციცებით
ფეხზე შემდგარის თოფითა,
ჰხედავს, რომ მოალაჯუნებს
კაცი ორ-კაპის ჯოხითა.
შავი რამ მოსთრავს პირ-თავქვე,
ქვიშა ქანავდა იმითა.
არას ამბობდა უცნობი,
სიტყვა არ მოსდის პირითა.
უპრჭყვინავს სალტა თოფისა,
ვით წვიმის ცვარი დილითა.
- ვინ ხარ, რა სულიერი ხარ,
რას იარები ამ დროსა?
- ვინ გინდა? მონადირე ვარ,
კაცს შენ ვერ გხედავ სანდოსა.

The slopes covered with ice;
It darkens and shrouds
The visible landscape.
Making the hunter cry out,
His track lost among cliffs,
Bringing joy to the wolf, the thief,
Those walkers in the dark.

II

High above, some stranger
Dislodges a rock from the cliff.
The traveller looks up,
Faced by a tall mountain.
He listens….after a moment
Hearing the hiss of sand.
He reaches for his gun:
It might be an enemy.
He looks about feverishly,
His weapon at the ready.
He sees someone burdened
With a double-headed staff.
He was dragging its dark weight,
That's why the sand hissed.
The stranger said not a word,
Not a sound came from his mouth,
The barrel of the gun gleaming
Like the dew after morning rain.
He asked: 'What kind of man are you?
Why are you wandering here at this hour?'
'What would you have? I'm a hunter.'
'You don't look like one to me.'

- რაობით სანდო არა ვარ?
სიტყვას რად ამბობ მცდარესა?
ვითომ, რომ დავხეტიალობ
შენებრ ამ კლდიან მხარესა?
მეც მონადირე გახლავარ,
დღეს-კი ვეხეტე უბრალოდ.
- წესია მონადირისა,
ხომ მაინც დაჰრჩი უვალოდ?
- ესეც ვალია, ძმობილო,
ძლივს-ლა დავათრევ ფეხებსა,
სულ დავიარე ჭიუხი,
არა ვსტოვებდი ხევებსა.
ზედ შავი ნისლი ჩამოწვა,
ნიავი მოსცა ძლიერი,
ხევებით შემომდმუოდა,
როგორაც მგელი მშიერი.
თვალ-წინ გზას ვეღარ ვირჩევდი,
კლდეზე გადვარდნას ვლამობდი,
ხამად ვარ, გეზი არ ვიცი,
ამით ძლიერა ვწვალობდი.
ბევრგან დავაფთხე ნადირი,
ცხადად ფეხის ხმა მესმოდა,
ან როცა გადაფრენილის
ჯიხვის რქა კლდეებს ესმოდა.
ის იყო გულის საკლავი,
თვალით ვერაფერს ვხედავდი,
სროლას, ან მოკვლას ვინ იტყვის,
წინ სვლას ვეღარა ვბედავდი.
უცნობი ახლოს მივიდა,
შორი-ახლოსა მდგომარე,

'Why should you not trust me?
Why are you suspicious?
Because I'm wandering perhaps
Like you across this mountain?
I am a hunter too,
And today I've hunted in vain.'
'So it goes with us hunters.
Would you live without trouble?'
'This also is trouble, brother,
I can barely move a step,
I've walked all these hills,
I traversed every ravine;
Black fog swirled around
Driven by a strong wind;
It howled through the ravines
Like a famished wolf.
I could barely see the road;
I tried to descend the cliff,
At a loss to know the way
I was struggling so fiercely.
I scared the beasts near and far,
I could hear their hooves clearly,
I could hear the rams clashing horns
As they fled along the cliff.
My heart sank at that
I could see nothing ahead;
Forget about the hunting,
I dared not take a step forward.'
The stranger standing close by
Came a little closer.
The traveller called out: 'Hunt on, then,
Don't complain, stay calm.'

"გამარჯვებაო" მისძახა,
"ნუ სჩივი, ნუ ხარ მწყრომარე".
- შენც გაგიმარჯოს, ძმობილო,
ჰხოცო ნადირი მხტომარე.
- აი, ნადირი, რას სჩივი? -
უჩვენა ჯიხვი რქიანი, -
მკვდარი, რქებ-გადაგდებული,
დადუმებული, ჭკვიანი.
თუ გინდა ეხლავ გავიყოთ,
როგორც ამხანაგთ, ორადა,
ჩიჩქიც არ მინდა მე მეტი,
გავინაწილოთ სწორადა.
ამაღამ ჩემთან წამოდი,
სახლი არ მიდგა შორადა.
სადაური ხარ, ძმობილო?
სახელიც მითხარ შენია.
ნუ სწუხარ, საზრდო შენთვისაც
დღეს უფალს გაუჩენია.
წილი გდებია შენაცა
ამ ჩემგან მოკლულს ჯიხვშია.
რად გიკვირს, არ გებუმრები,
არც გეფერები პირშია.
მაშ, თუ ეს ასე არ არის,
რად შამეფეთე ამ დროსა?!
შაჰრცხვეს, ჩემს თავად, ვინც შენა
ნაწილი დაგიკარგოსა.
რა გქვიან? სახელი მითხარ,
ხევსური სჩანხარ იერით.
- ნუნუა მქვიან, ძმისაო,
გადმოხვეწილი ჭიელით, -

'Good hunting to you too, brother,
Kill a host of those agile creatures.'
'Here's one. So why complain?'
He showed him a horned ram,
Lying dead, one with curving horns.
'A cunning one, but silent now.
If you want we'll share it,
Equal shares, like comrades,
I'll not take more than my own,
Let's share it justly,
Come home with me tonight,
My dwelling is nearby.
Where do you come from, brother?
Tell me your name as well!
Don't' worry, God has found
Food for you too today.
You shall have your share
In this ram I've slain,
Don't look surprised, it's no jest,
And I'm not seeking favours.
If it was not meant to be,
Why would you meet me, now?
It would be a shame
If you lost your share,
Who are you? Tell me your name.
Your looks seem Khesvurian.'
'I am called, Nunua, brother,
A wanderer in the hills.'

იცრუა ზვიადაურმა,
თვისი სახელი დამალა.
რა ქნას? მის სახელს იცნობენ,
ქისტებს ბევრს სისხლი ავალა;
ბევრს ქისტს მოაჭრა მარჯვენა,
უდროდ საფლავში ჩალალა.
- შენი სახელიც მასწავლე,
ჩემი ხომ გითხარ მართლადა.
- ჯოყოლა მქვიან, ძოზილო,
ალხასტაისძე გვარადა;
არ მოგვიხდება, ერთურთში
სიტყვა ვიუბნოთ მცდარადა.
სახლი აქ ჯარეგას მიდგა,
ქავი და ციხე კარადა.
ამაღამ ჩემთან წამოდი,
მე გაგიძღვები თავადა.
თუ კარგად არ დაგიხვდები,
არც დაგიხვდები ავადა.
ხვალ თითონ იცი, ძმოზილო,
საითაც გინდა, იარე.
ზოგს მე გიამბობ ჩემს დარდსა,
ზოგიც შენ გამიზიარე.
- საცა არ მიხნავ, ძმოზილო,
იქ ვმკო - ეს სადაურია?
ყელი მოგიჭრავ ჯიხვისთვის,
ფეხებიც ჩატყყაულია.
გესტუმრო, უარს არ გეტყვი,
გიშველი ჯიხვის ზიდვასა,
წილს-კი არ მოგთხოვ, იცოდე,
თავს არ ვაკადრეზ იმასა.

47

But Zviadauri lied,
He concealed his true name.
What could he do? He was notorious,
He owed a debt of blood to many Kists,
He had cut the right hand of many Kists,
Sent them to an untimely grave.
'Tell me your name, too,
Now I have told you mine.'
'Mine is Jokhala, brother,
My last name, Alkhastaidze;
It would not do for us
To tell lies.
My house is nearby,
With doors like a fortress.
Come home with me tonight,
I'll take you there myself.
If I'm not the perfect host
I'll not treat you ill, at least.
Tomorrow, take your own way,
Go wherever you wish.
I'll tell you some of my troubles,
You can share some of yours.'
  'Lead me wherever you wish, brother,
I long to be there – How far is it?
You've cut the ram's throat,
And skinned its legs too.
I'll not refuse to visit,
I'll help carry the ram too
I don't ask for a share, you know,
I'd not dishonour myself like that.'

შამოატყავეს ნადირი,
წავიდნენ ჯარეგაშია,
ბევრი იუბნეს ამბავი,
ერთურთს გაეცნენ გზაშია.

III

მივიდნენ, კოშკები დაჩნდა,
აქა-იქ ჰყეფენ ძაღლები;
კარებში იცქირებიან
ცნობისმოყვარე ბალღები.
დაეტყო ცხადად კლდის მსგავსად
სიპით ნაგები სახლები.
- აი, ეს ჩემი ოჯახი,
ჩემი ციხე და სახლია;
მობძანდი, როგორც ძმა ძმასთან.
ნათლიმამასთან - ნათლია.
ცოლს დაუძახა ჯოყოლამ:
- გამოიხედე კარშია! -
ეტყობა თავმოწონება
მასპინძელს საუბარშია.
სდგანან დერეფანს, უცდიან...
ცეცხლი ჰკრთებოდა ღველფზედა,
ჩონგურს უკრავდა, დროული
კაცი რამ უჯდა გვერდზედა.
დაჰმღერდა გმირობისასა,
მამა-პაპათა ცდისასა:
როგორ არბევდნენ ფშავ-ხევსურთ,
სისხლს არ არჩენდენ ძმისასა;
ყველგან მადლობას სწირავენ
მარჯვენას კაის ყმისასა.

Between them they skinned the ram,
And carried it to the house,
They exchanged many stories,
Grew acquainted as they went.

III

The turrets came in sight,
Dogs were barking;
From the doorways
Curious children were gazing;
The stone-built houses
Seemed like giant boulders.
'Look, here are my family,
My fortress, my home;
Welcome, as brother to brother,
As godson to godfather.'
Jokhala called to his wife:
'Come see who's at the door!'
Pride was apparent
In the host's conversation.
As they stood in the hallway, waiting…
The fire smouldered in the hearth,
An old man played on a lyre,
A man sitting near to him,
Sang of heroes
Of ancestral wars:
How they sacked Pshav-Khevsureti,
In vengeance for the blood of their brother;
They celebrate everywhere
The hand of a righteous man.

გამოჩნდა ქალი ლამაზი,
შავის ტანსაცმლით მოსილი,
როგორაც ალყა ტანადა,
ვარსკვლავი ციდამ მოცლილი.
- აი, სტუმარი მოგგვარე, -
ღვთის წყალობაა ჩვენზედა, -
როგორც დაგვხვდები, დიაცო,
ეხლა ჰჯიდია შენზედა.
ქალმა სალამი მიართო:
- სტუმარო, მოხვედ მშვიდობით!
- შენდაც მშვიდობა, გაცოცხლოს
თავის ქმრითა და წილობით!
სტუმარს აბჯარი წაუღო,
მიიპატიჟეს შინაო;
ქალი მისდევდა უკანა,
ჯოყოლა მიდის წინაო;
თან მისდევს ზვიადაური,
ძმობილი გაიჩინაო.

IV
კაცი რომ სჩანდა სახლშია,
ჭადარ-შერთული, ხნიერი,
წამოდგა ისიც ფეხზედა,
როგორც კლდის ვეფხვი, ძლიერი.
სტუმრად მოსული უცნობი,
სტუმარს პატივს სცემს სხვისასა,
ფეხზე ადგომა წესია,
წესს ვერ დაარღვევს მთისასა.
მაგრამ, როს ნახა უცნობი,
ფერი დაედო მგლისაო;
ადვილად აიცნობოდა,

Then a beautiful woman appeared,
Dressed in black,
Slender as a willow tree,
Like a star descended to earth.
'See, I have brought you a guest.'
'Mercy be to God.'
How you will treat our guest, wife,
That is for you to say.
The woman welcomed him in:
'Guest, may peace be upon you!'
'You too, may you have peace
And your husband and children!'
She took the guest's weapons,
They invited him in;
The woman following behind,
Jokhala leading;
Zviadauri following
His new brother.

IV

The man who sat by the hearth,
Grey-haired, elderly,
He rose now to his feet,
Like a powerful tiger on a cliff-top.
An old man, there as a guest,
Must respect the guest of another,
To rise to one's feet is expected,
He must follow the mountain ways.
But on seeing the stranger,
He took on the mask of the wolf;
They were evident,

რასაც ფიქრობდა ისაო.
არ ეჭაშნიკა დროულს ქისტს
დანახვა უცხოს ყმისაო.
გული სცემს ბრაზმორეული,
სახეც არ ჰმალავს ამასა,
ხანჯრისკე ხელი მიუდის,
ჩუმად სინჯავდა დანასა,
მაგრამ სტუმარი სხვის სახლში
ვერ გაჰშლის ხათაბალასა.
ადგა და ჩუმად გავიდა,
თითზე იკბინა მწარედა,
სამჯერ ჩაიკრა გულს ხელი,
როცა გავიდა გარედა.
წავიდა. კარი-კარ დადის,
ენასა ჰლესავს შხამითა:
"ქისტებო, ჩვენი მოსისხლე
შემოგვეპარა ღამითა.
სჩანს, რო ჯოყოლა ვერ იცნობს,
არ უნახია თვალითა
ეგ ჩვენი ამომგდებელი,
ჩვენი მრზეველი ძალითა;
გაუმაძღარი მუდამ ჭამს
ჩვენის სისხლით და ძვალითა
დღეს ჩვენს ხელთ არის, ვეცადოთ,
ვაგემოთ გემო მწარია,
მაგათ მოკლული ამ ზაფხულს
გვყავს უპატრონო მკვდარია.
სთქვით, თუ არ ვამბობ სიმართლეს,
თუ ჩემი სიტყვა მცდარია?!
გაიგოს ჩვენმა დუშმანმაც,

The thoughts in his mind,
The aged Kist felt no pleasure,
On seeing this stranger.
His heart throbbed with anger,
And his face betrayed it,
His hand drifted to his sword,
And he checked his knife, covertly,
But a guest cannot start a quarrel
In another man's house.
He rose and exited quietly,
Biting his finger in bitterness,
He beat at his chest three times,
As he stepped outside.
He left and went from house to house,
Sharpening his tongue with poison:
'Our deadly enemy, you Kists,
Walks with you, disguised, in the night.
It seems, Jokhala fails to know him
His eyes have not pierced the disguise.
He is the decimator of our people,
Attacking us with violence,
Forever insatiable in his desire
For our blood and bone.
Today he is in our hands, let's see
If we can make him taste the bitterness
Of those Khevsur killed this summer;
We have unburied dead.
Tell me, if I fail of the truth,
If my words are in error!
Make our enemy know too,

არ გვაქვს უჯიშო გვარია.
მიკვირს ჯოყოლას ჭკვისაგან,
მტერს რად გაუღო კარია,
ვისა ჰმასპინძლობს ჭკვათხელი,
ცნობაზე რად არ არია?!
ცხვირიდამ უნდა ვადინოთ
ზვიადაურსა ძმარია,
თუ არა, დიაცთ დაუთმოთ
ჩვენი ხმალი და ფარია".
აღელვდენ ქისტის შვილები,
ყველამ შაიბა ხმალია,
აღელვდა მთელი სოფელი:
ბალღი, კაცი და ქალია.
უნდა შასწიროს თავის მკვდარს
ზვიადაურის თავია;
უნდა მტრის საფლავზე დაკლან,
როგორაც წესი არია.
გაგზავნეს ერთი მზვერავი,
თან აბარებენ ჩუმადა,
მივიდეს ჯოყოლასთანა
მეზობლურადა, ძმურადა;
სოფლის განზრახვა არა-გზით
მას არ ჩაუგდოს ყურადა.
ივახშმოს, იმუსაითფოს,
გაიგოს სტუმრის ლოგინი;
ღამე დაესხნენ, შაკონონ,
არ უნდესთ ბევრი ლოდინი.
მივიდა მოყურიადე
ლაქარდიანის ენითა,
სახელს ულოცავს ჯოყოლას,

That we are not basely born.
I am surprised at Jokhala,
Why open the door to an enemy,
Who is this guest? The idiot,
Why does he not see?
We must bring bitterness
To Zviadauri's nostrils,
If not then let the women
Wield our shields and swords.'
Even the Kists' children were stirred,
Everyone strapped on a sword,
The entire village was stirred –
Man, woman, and child.
They must sacrifice the life
Of Zviadauri to their dead;
They must kill him on his enemy's grave
As is the custom.
To send a spy,
Instructing him in secret,
To go to Jokhala,
Like a neighbour and a brother;
Not to divulge in any way
The villagers' intent.
To eat and to converse,
To discover where the guest will sleep;
To assault him at night, and bind him,
Needs little debate.
The spy arrives
With ingratiating tongue
He blesses Jokhala's name,

ლაღობს, არ არის წყენითა.
ხალვათობს, ამბობს ამბებსა,
ენას აკვესებს კვესითა.
ვინ იცის, გული სავსე აქვს
გველის შხამით და გესლითა.
ივახშმეს. თვისი სტუმარი
მასპინძელს მოსწონს გულითა.
"კარგი ვაჟკაცი ეტყობა", -
ფიცულობს თავის რჯულითა:
"ეს ერთი ცნობა, ხვალ ძმობა,
ერთად შევთვისდეთ სულითა"...
მიიპატიჟა სამძღრედ,
დაუთმო თვისი ლაჩანი.
- არაო, - სტუმარი ეტყვის, -
არ მინდა ლეიბ-საბანი.
მე დერეფანში დავსწვები,
შინ ძილს არც-კი ვარ ჩვეული...
ასრულდა მისი წადილი,
გულიდამ ამოწეული,
მოყურიადეს ეს უნდა,
ამად არს აქ მოწვეული.
წავიდა გახარებული,
შეატყობინა ყველასა.
მამლის საჯდომი თუ იცის,
მეტი რა უნდა მელასა?!

V
- რა ამბავია, დიაცო?
ხმალი მინდა და ხანჯარი!

He speaks freely, gives no offence.
He jests and tells stories,
He strikes sparks with his tongue.
Who could know his heart was full
Of the venom of a deadly snake.
They dined. The host
Admired his guest with all his heart.
'He's a brave man, you can tell,'
He swore by his cult,
'Meeting today, tomorrow as brothers
Let us be one in spirit.'
He invited him to rest,
And showed him to his own bed.
His guest refused it, 'No,'
I want neither mattress nor blanket.
I'll sleep in the entrance way,
I'm not used to sleeping inside…
He had achieved the goal
Aimed at in his heart,
This is what the spy desires,
It's why he made his way there.
And he left joyfully,
To spread the news around.
If the fox knows where the cockerel roosts,
What more can he wish!

V

'Wife, what's all this confusion?
Bring me my sword and sabre!

სახუმრო საქმე არაა,
თავზე დაგვესხა მტრის ჯარი!
ნამდვილ აკლებას გვიპირობს,
გვდალატობს ჩვენი სტუმარი;
ძმობით და მეგობრობითა
შემოგვაპარა ლაშქარი!
სუ, დაიცადე!.. მოვსტყუვდი...
ჩვენი ქისტები არიან.
რისთვის მოვიდნენ ამ დროსა,
რას ბჯობენ, ვის რა სწადიან?!
ყური დაუგდე კარგადა,
კაცისა მესმის ხრიალი.
რა მქისე ხმაურობაა,
რა საზარელი გრიალი!
ჩემს სტუმარსა ჰკვლენ, სწორედა,
უდგასთ ხანჯრების პრიალი.
უყყურე უნამუსოთა,
ჩემს ოჯახს როგორ ჰქელავენ!
ჩაიგდეს ჩემი კაცობა,
ფეხს ქვეშ ტყლაპივით სთელავენ,
გავიგო, აბა, წავიდე,
რაზე, რისთვისა ჰღელავენ?!
ეს სთქვა ჯოყოლამ, წამოდგა,
ხელ-ხანჯრიანი წავიდა.
გააღო სახლის კარები,
შეუპოვარად გავიდა.
- რას სჩადით? - შემოუქახა: -
ვის სტუმარს ჰზოჩავთ თოჯითა?
რად სტეხთ საუფლო ჩვენს წესსა,
თავს ლაფს რად მასხამთ კოკითა?

59

This is no trivial skirmish,
The whole enemy force is attacking!
They are out to destroy us,
Our guest has betrayed us;
Beneath brotherhood and friendship
He's concealed an army!
Hush! Wait! I am wrong…
They are our Kists.
Why are they here, now;
What are they crying, what do they want?
Listen, carefully,
I can hear a man screaming.
What a dire sound,
What a dreadful deed!
They are slaughtering my guest
With their glittering swords.
Look at those ruthless ones,
How they trample through my home!
They have my manhood in their hands,
And they crush it as they crush the grapes.
Let me go and see,
What has stirred them so?…'
So saying, Jokhala rose
And gripping his sword in his hand,
He opened the doors of his house,
And stepped out defiantly.
'Why are you here? He cried,
'Whose guest do you bind with rope?
Why do you break our sovereign law,
Why do you drench my head with mud?

ჩემს სჯულსა ვფიცავ, სისხლს დავღვრი,
განანებთ ბრიყვულს ქცევასა,
განანებთ, თუმცა ძმანი ხართ,
ჩემის კაცობის ქელვასა!..
- რას ამბობ, შტერო, რას ამბობ?
რად არ მოდიხარ ცნებასა?
მოსისხლე სტუმრის გულისთვის
ძუძუს ვინ მოსჭრის დედასა?! -
შემოუძახეს ქისტებმა
ერთხმად, ძლიერად, ჭექითა: -
შენ და შენს სტუმარს, ორივეს
ერთად გადგისვრით ბექია.
თემს რაც სწადიან, მას იზამს
თავის თემობის წესითა.
მთელის ქისტების ამომგდე
სტუმრად რადა გყავ სახლშია?
ზვიადაურის სახელი
ბავშვმაც კი იცის მთაშია.
ეს იყო მუდამ, ჭკვათხელო,
ჩვენის გაჯლეტის ცდაშია,
მგლურად რო გვეტევებოდა,
რო გვიჯდებოდა გზაშია.
ჯოყოლა ცოტას შეფიქრდა,
პირს სინანული წაესო,
თითქოს ნატყორცი ისარი
ზედ გულის კოვზზე დაესო.
- თვით ამან მოჰკლა შენი ძმა
არყიანებში თოფითა,
ჩვენ ვიცნობთ მაგის სახესა,
გადალესულსა ცოფითა.

I swear by my religion, I'll shed blood,
You will regret your vile conduct,
You'll regret this, though you are my brothers,
Trampling like this on my manhood!...'
'What do you mean, you fool,
Have you lost your wits?
Over a deadly guest, an enemy
Who would cut off the breasts of his own mother!'
So the Kists cried,
Shouting, all at once, loud as thunder
'You and your guest, will both
Be hurled from the cliffs together.
Whatever the tribe must do, it will
According to the tribe's rules.
This decimator of all Kisteti
Why do you treat him as your guest?
In the mountains, even a child
Knows this Zviadauri's name.
You fool, he's forever trying,
To exterminate us all.
He attacks us like a wolf,
He ambushes us on the trail.'
Jokhala thought deeply,
His face filled with regret,
As if an arrow had been fired,
Into the very centre of his heart.
'It was he who killed your brother,
With his gun, in the birch-wood.
We know his face,
Fierce with rage.

"გახლავართ ზვიადაური!" -
ჩამოგვკიოდა გორითა;
სულ კარგად ვიცით, ცხადადა,
თვალს ვადევნებდით შორითა.
აავსო ფშავ-ხევსურეთი
აქით წასხმულის ძროხითა.
უკან გაუდგა ლაშქარსა
ფეხმარდი, ლეგის ჩოხითა.
თავს რად იმურტლავ, ბეჩავო,
გაუმაძღარის ღორითა?
გული როგორ არ გერევა
მაგასთან ჯდომა-ყოფნითა?!
- ეგ მართალია, იქნება...
რა უნდა მითხრათ მაგითა,
მითც ვერ მიაბამთ ჩემს გულსა
თქვენს გულისთქმასთან ძაფითა.
დღეს სტუმარია ეგ ჩემი,
თუნდ ზღვა ემართოს სისხლისა,
მითაც მე ვერ ვულალატებ,
ვფიცავ ღმერთს, ქმნილი იმისა.
მე გთხოვ გაუშვა, მუსაო,
ნუ სტანჯავ უდიერადა,
როცა გასცდება ჩემს ოჯახს,
იქ მოეპყარით ავადა.
ვის გაუყიდავ სტუმარი?
ქისტეთს სად თქმულა ამბადა?
რა დავაშავე ისეთი,
რომ მომიხედით კარადა?
თვის რჯული დაგვიწყებიათ,
მიტომ იქცევით მცდარადა;

"I am here, I, Zviadauri!"
He screamed from above;
We heard him clearly,
We were watching him from afar.
He filled Pshav-Khevsureti
With cattle he stole from us.
He stood behind the army,
Swift-footed, wearing a grey chokha.
Why do you shame yourself, you wretch,
For this insatiable creature?
How can you sit near him,
Without vomiting in his face?'
'All that may be true…
But what are you trying to say,
You can't tie my heart
To your wishes with a thread.
He is my guest, this day,
Though he owes me a sea of blood,
I cannot betray him.
I swear it, by God, his creator.
I ask you to loose him, Musa,
Not to torment him further,
When he leaves my household,
Then you may do as you wish.
Who has ever betrayed a guest,
In Kisteti, even in story?
What have I done, then,
That you are all at my door?
You forget the rules of your own cult,
That is why you act so wrongly;

ჩემს ოჯახს პასუხს რით აძლევთ?
სახლში ხართ, განა შარადა!
ვაი თქვენ, ქისტის შვილებო,
მომდგარნო ჩემს კარს ჯარადა!
უიარაღოს აწვალებთ,
გული რასა ჰგრძნობს თავადა?
მუსა (ჯოყოლას)
შენაც ამასთან შაგკონავთ,
თემის პირს რომ სტეხ, თავხედო!
ჩვენის ნარჩევის დარღვევა
შენ როგორ უნდა გაჰბედო?
აჰყეფდი ქოფაკივითა,
აბდა-უბდაობ შტერადა;
ამ გიაურის გულისთვის
ძმებსაც ეპყრობი მტერადა.
არ იცი, რომ შენი საქმეც
დღეიდგან წავა ცერადა?!
ჯოყოლა (მუსას)
რაო? ქოფაკო?! შენ ამბობ?
ახლა ძაღლადაც გამხადე?! -
იძრო ხანჯარი, მუსასა
გულში უმარჯვა ვადამდე.
- უყურე თვით ძაღლს, უყურე,
გამითამამდა სადამდე!
ჩემის კაცობის დამქცევნო,
ლანძღვასაც მემართლებითა?
ალლახსა ვფიცავ, გაგმუსრავთ,
მანამ ამკაფავთ ხმლებითა,
გრისხავდესით ცა-ქვეყნის მადლი,
უსამართლობას შვრებითა!

What would you say to my family?
You are in my house, not outside!
Woe to you, children of Kists,
Who come to my door in force!
You attack an unarmed man,
How does that make you feel?'
Musa (to Jokhala)
'We will bind you too,
For shaming the tribe, you wretch!
Will you dare to disobey
What we order?
You're barking like some sheep-dog,
You are talking foolish nonsense;
On behalf of this non-believer,
Treating your brothers as the enemy,
Do you realise your own life
Will be filled now with misfortune!'

Jokhala (to Musa):

'What? Do you call me a dog?
Then I'll act like one, too!'
He drew his dagger,
And thrust it to the hilt into Musa's heart.
'Look, here is the true dog,
See how bold he grows with me!
You tramplers on my manhood,
Do you dare to curse me?
I swear, by Allah, I'll slay you,
Before you can murder me with your sabres
May the wrath of land and sky show you no mercy,
For the unjust thing you do!'

- რა ქნა უღმერთომ, რა ქნაო,
გაგიჟდა, ჭკვაზე მცდარია... -
ჯოყოლას თავზე დაეცა
მთლი ქისტების ჯარია,
ხელი შაუკრეს... არ მისცეს
ნება, ეხმარა ხმალია...
ხელ-ფეხშაკრული დერეფანს
დააგდეს, როგორც მკვდარია.
წყევლა ხალხისა ჭექაა,
ნაფურთხი - წვიმის ცვარია.
წამოიყვანეს დაჭრილი,
ზვიადაურიც სტანია.
რას ამბობს ზვიადაური?
სახე რადა აქვს მტკნარია?
ბოღმა მიტომ ჰკლავს ვაჟკაცსა,
რომ ხელთ არა აქვს ხმალია:
"ჩამიგდეთ ხელში, ძაღლებო,
კარგი დაგიდგათ დარია".
ამას ამბობდა დინჯადა,
სხვად არას მოუბარია.
მიჰყავდათ სასაფლაოზე,
სადაც ქისტების მკვდარია,
უნდა თავის მკვდარს შესწირონ,
რომ იქ უზიდოს წყალია,
მსახურად ჰყავდეს, მორჩილად,
და გაუბანდოს ჯღანია...

VI
სოფლისა გალმა გორია,
დამწვარი, ქვიშიანია.

'Oh God, what has he done,
He's given way to madness…'
Jokhala was attacked
By the whole force of Kists,
They tied his hands…they made sure
He could not wield his sword…
They threw him into the hallway
His hands and feet bound like a corpse.
The people's condemnation is thunder,
Their saliva, the moisture of rain.
They seized the wounded man too,
Zviadauri….
What does Zviadauri say,
Why is his face like a stoic's?
Grief is killing that brave man,
Because his hand lacks a sword:
'You have seized me, you dogs,
A fortunate day for you!'
He said this quite calmly,
And he said nothing more.
They were dragging him to the graveyard,
Where the Kists were buried;
As a sacrifice to the dead,
To bear water for them there,
To obey them as their servant,
And wash their feet…

VI

On the far side of the village was a hill,
Scorched, and dusty;

ზევრი წევს იქა ვაჟკაცი,
გულ-ლომი, ჯიშიანია.
ძირს მისდგამს ზექი მდუმარე,
ნაღვარი, თიხიანია.
ხმალ-ხანჯრის, თოფის მხმარეთი
არა სმგერს გული მაგარი;
იმათ სჭამს მიწა უენო,
სასტიკი, გაუმაძღარი;
მასში ეშლება ყველასა
ადამიანის იერი...
ვერ გვიხსნის სიკვდილის ბჯღალით
ძალა, ვერც სიტყვა ცბიერი.
ბუნების ცოდვა ესაა,
მუდამ საწყინო ჩემია:
ავსა და კარგსა ყველას ჰკლავს,
არავინ გადურჩენია.
ყველა მგზავრთათვის ინთქმევა,
როცა იღუპვის გემია!..
მზე ჯერ არ ამოსულიყო,
ნამს ჯერ ბალახზე ეძინა,
არ დაებერა ნიავსა,
დაბლა არ ჩამოეფინა,
ურიცხვი კაცი და ქალი
ჭალაზე შამოეფინა.
მოჰყავდა ზვიადაური
ხელშეკონილი გროვასა,
ყველას უხარის მის მოკვლა,
ან ვინ დაიწყებს გლოვასა?!
სიკვდილი ყველას გვაშინებს,
სხვას თუ ჰკვლენ, ცქერა გვწადიან;

Many brave men lay there,
Lion-hearted, nobly bred.
The silent hillside sloped below,
A torrent flowing through clay.
Those who wielded sword and gun
Their strong hearts no longer beat;
The voiceless ground devours them,
Harsh and insatiable;
Everyone thinks of it
As the very likeness of a human being...
Strength cannot save us from mortal fate
Nor cunning words.
This is Nature's deep flaw,
That always offends my mind:
It kills everyone, good or bad,
And no-one survives in the end.
When the ship is wrecked
Every passenger is drowned!...
The sun had not yet risen,
The dew still rested on the grass,
The breeze had not yet blown,
Had not spread from above.
Countless men and women
Were gathered there.
Zviadauri was brought
Hands bound before the crowd,
All are eager for his slaughter,
Yet who among them would grieve?
Death terrifies us all,
When others are killed, we long to watch;

კაცნი ვერ ჰგრძნობენ ბევრჯელა,
როგორ დიდს ცოდვას სჩადიან.
რამდენი ავსული ვიცი,
წარბშეუბრელად დადიან;
თავის მტანჯველის შემუსრვა
ან კი ვის არა სწადიან?!

VII
აი საფლავიც ქისტისა,
ხალხი მოერტყა გარსაო,
მოლა მოჰყვება ლოცვასა,
იხსენებს თავის მკვდარსაო:
"ნუ იტანჯები, დარლაო,
ნუ შეიწუხებ თავსაო,
მოვსდეგით შენი მომძმენი
შენის სამარის კარსაო,
მსხვერპლსაცა გწირავთ, იხარე,
არ გაჭმევთ მტრისა ჯავრსაო".
- ძაღლ იყოს თქვენის მკვდრისადა! -
ვაჟკაცი იძებს ხმასაო,
ბეწვს იშლის ბრაზმორეული,
როგორაც ვეფხვი - თმასაო.
საკირის ცეცხლი ედება
სამსხვერპლოს გულის-თქმასაო.
რა მოსდრეკს წარბ-დაღრუბლილსა,
ქედ-ჩაჯანგებულს მთასაო!
აქცევენ ზვიადაურსა,
ყელში აბჯენენ ხმალსაო:
"დარლასამც შაეწირები",
ყველა დასძახის მასაო.

71

Most of the time men do not feel
The wickedness of their actions.
There are so many sinful souls,
Who live their lives without remorse;
Yet who does not wish to destroy
One who harms them?

VII

Here is the grave of a Kist,
Surrounded by the crowd.
Moollah begins to pray,
Remembering his dead:
'Suffer, no more, Darda,
Nor be troubled,
Here are your brothers
At the door of your grave,
Be joyful, we sacrifice to you,
No longer swallow your anger against your foe,
May this dog die for you!'
The stranger's voice is heard,
His hackles are rising,
His hair like a tiger's.
Lime is burning
In the victim's inner core.
Will this subdue his rage,
A blade with a rusted edge!
They fall upon Zviadauri,
Set the sword at his throat:
'We sacrifice you to Darla!'
They all cry.

"მაღლ იყოს თქვენის მკვდრისადა!" -
უპასუხებდა ხალხსაო.
არ იდრიკება ვაჟკაცი,
არ შეიხრიდა წარბსაო.
გაოცდენ ქისტის შვილები,
ხალხი დგებოდა ყალხსაო.
"ლამის რომ არ შაეწიროს,
ერთი უყურეთ მაღლსაო!"
ჰყვირიან, თანაც ნელ-ნელა
ყელში ურჩობენ ხმალსაო.
"მაღლ იყოს", ყელში ამზობდა,
მანამ მოსჭრიდენ თავსაო!
"უცქირეთ, ერთი უცქირეთ,
არ ახამხამებს თვალსაო!"
სიცოცხლე ჰქრება, სისხლი დის, -
ზვიადაური კვდებოდა,
გული ვერ მოჰკლა მტრის ხელმა,
გული გულადვე რჩებოდა.
და ამ სურათის მნახველი
ერთი დიაცი ზნდებოდა,
ცრემლებს ჰმალავდა ლამაზი,
ხალხზე უკანა დგებოდა.
მიშველებასა ჰლამობდა:
"ნუ ჰკლავთ!" ეძახის გულიო,
ფიქრობდა ბრაზმორეული:
ნეტავი მომცა ცულიო,
ნეტავი ნებას მაძლევდეს
დედაკაცობის რჯულიო,
რომ ეგ ვაცოცხლო, სხვას ყველას
გავაფრთხობინო სულიო.

(Zviadauri): 'Your dead are the dogs!'
He shouted to the crowd.
A brave man, defiant.
Unwavering, his brow.
The Kists were confounded,
The crowd reared up.
'He refuses to die,
Behold, this dog!'
They are shouting and as they do
Slowly driving in the sword.
'You are the dogs!' he murmured in his throat
Before they severed his head!
'Look at him, look,
Not a blink from his eyes!'
Life is ebbing, he is bleeding,
Zviadauri is dying,
But an enemy hand could not quench his heart,
His heart was still his heart…
And witnessing all this
One lovely woman melted,
Hiding her tears
Standing there, behind the crowd,
She wanted to aid him:
Her heart screamed: 'Don't kill him!'
She was thinking, angrily:
'I wish I had a scythe,
I wish the female cult
Gave me the right,
To grant him life
In exchange for all these souls.

ნეტავი იმას, ვინაცა
მაგის მკლავზედა წვებოდა,
ვისიცა მკერდი, აწ კრული,
მაგის გულ-მკერდსა სწვდებოდა!
ნეტავი იმას ოდესმე
ქმრის ტრფობა გაუცვდებოდა?!
ქისტები გაწყრენ, იტკიცეს:
ვერ აუსრულდათ წადილი,
ვერ გაუკეთეს თავის მკვდარს
მის შესაფერი სადილი.
დაკლულმა დაჰკლა მათ გული
და გაუცრუა ქადილი.
შეურაცხყოფილთ უნდოდათ
ერთად გაექროთ ხანჯრები
და გაექეთათ მკვდრის გვამზე
სისხლით ნაღები ფანჯრები.
მაგრამ ვერ ჰბედვენ, სცხვენიანთ:
"ცოდვაა!" - ყველა ჰფიქრობდა.
ხალხის გული და გონება
სასინანულოდ მიჰქროდა.
სთქვეს, როცა სახლში გაბრუნდენ,
თავ-თავქვე ჩამოდიოდენ:
ხომ მაგას არ მოვუკლავდით
მტრებს, ავს რომ არ სჩადიოდენ?
კარგი ვაჟკაცი ყოფილა,
ყველა ალლახსა ჰფიცავდა,
იმიტომ ვეფხვებრ გვებრძოდა,
თავის მიწა-წყალს იცავდა.
მაგრამ მტერს მტრულად მოექე,
თვითონ უფალმა ბრძანაო,

I wish I were the one
Who might sleep in his arms,
Whose breast, now damned,
Lay on his breast,
Would that one ever tire
Of her husband's love!'
The Kists were angered, shamed:
Their wish was not fulfilled,
They could not make a fitting sacrifice
To the dead;
Their victim slew their hearts
And diminished their joy.
Ashamed they desired
To wield their swords as one
And make of the corpse
Ribbons stained with blood.
But they did not dare from shame:
And 'Shameful!' all were thinking.
Their hearts and minds
Vexed and troubled.
As they headed home,
Heads low, descending, they said:
'We'd not have killed him
If as an enemy he'd not harmed us.
He was a brave man',
All swore to Allah,
'That's why he fought like a tiger,
Defending the honour of his land.'
But "treat your enemy with harshness"
God himself commands us,

ის სჯობს, რაც მალე ვეცდებით,
გულში ჩავურჩჭოთ დანაო.
წავიდნენ. ზვიადაური
ზეზე გაწირეს ტიალად.
თუნდა მაღლებმა ათრიონ,
ფრინველთა ჯიჯგნონ ზიარად;
არ შაეწირა, ეგდოსო,
ეგეც ეყოფა ზიანად.
ამას იძახდენ ქისტები
თავმოწონებით, ხმიანად.
ამ ხმასვე იმეორებდენ
ბნელი ხევები მთიანად.
ჩამოდგა საღამოს ჟამი,
მთიდამ მზის სხივი ჩამოხდა,
სიბნელე მოიპარება,
სინათლეს სული ამოჰხდა.
დადგნენ, სულ დადგნენ მზის სხივნი,
აღარ ელავდა ქვიშაო;
აღარსადა სჩანს, გამქრალა
თეთრი თმა შავის მთისაო;
ნაღვლით ნაქარგი, ნაქსოვი
სახე იმ სალის კლდისაო,
რო მუდამ მგლოვიარეა,
ცრემლი აწკარა სდისაო.
სიკვდილსა გლოვა უხდება,
მკვდარს ძმას - ტირილი დისაო,
ტყესა - ხარ-ირმის ნაფრენი,
ზოგ დროს - ყმუილი მგლისაო.
ვაჟკაცსა - ომში სიკვდილი,
ხელში - ნატეხი ხმლისაო,

The sooner then must we
Drive a knife into their hearts.'
They abandoned Zviadauri's
Corpse there, alone;
For the dogs to drag at him,
Birds to tear and dismember him;
'He was no sacrifice, let him rot there
That too is no less harm.'
The Kists proclaimed this
Proudly, in loud voices.
And their voices were echoed
By the mountains' dark ravines.
Night fell,
Light faded from the heights,
Darkness entered stealthily
The sun sank to rest.
The sunlight faded,
The sand no longer shining;
No longer seen now, vanished,
The white hair of the black summits.
Embroidered, veined with sorrows,
The face of those rocks,
That are forever grieving,
With pure streams like tears.
For death, mourning is fitting,
For a dead brother, a sister's weeping,
For the forest, the stag's trail,
Or the howling of wolves,
For a brave man death in battle,
Shattered sword in hand.

ომს - ლხინი გამარჯვებულთა
და დამარცხება მტრისაო.
ზვიადაურსა გლოვობდა
შფოთვა და ზორგვნა წყლისაო,
ნიავად ჩამონადენი
ოხვრა მაღალის მთისაო.
ცრემლი ნისლების ჯარისა
ნაბრძანებია ღვთისაო.
და წყაროს პირზე დიაცი, -
ტურფა, ლამაზი, - ქისტისა,
შუბლზე და მკერდზე წყალს ისხამს,
დრო და დრო გული მისდისა.
ზევრი იტირა ჩუმადა,
თუმცა დრო და დრო ჰკრთებოდა,
ზვიადაურის სიკვდილი
თვალებში ელანდებოდა.
სტიროდა, მაგრამ ტირილი
არ იყო, ეხათრებოდა:
ერთ მხრივ ხათრი აქვს თემისა,
მეორით - ღმერთი აშინებს,
ქისტეთის მტრისა მოზარეს
თავს რისხვას გადმოადინებს.
ეს ფიქრი გონებისაა,
გული თავისას შვრებოდა,
კაცის კაცურად სიკვდილი
გულიდამ არა ჰქრებოდა.
ქალის გულს იგი სურათი
შიგ გაეყარა ისრადა;
იმან დაადვა ლამაზსა
დაკლულის გლოვა კისრადა.

For war, the victory feast
With the enemy defeated.
Zviadauri was mourned
By the fret and fall of water,
The moan from the tall mountain
Freed on the breeze,
Tears from the ranks of mist
Ordained by God.
And by the stream, a woman,
Fine, a beauty of Kist,
Pours water over her breast and forehead,
Fainting from time to time.
She cried for a long time, quietly,
Though now and then she trembled,
The death of Zviadauri
Would appear before her eyes.
She was crying without tears,
Constrained by respect:
Respect for the tribe on the one hand
On the other, her fear of God.
Grieving for an enemy
Would bring their anger upon her.
The thought was in her mind,
But her heart took its own path,
The man's heroic death,
Was etched on her heart.
That scene had pierced
The woman's heart like an arrow,
Forcing this beauty
To mourn the slaughtered one.

სიბნელეს უცდის, მივიდეს,
ლამით იტიროს მკვდარიო;
იმას აღარა ჰფიქრობდა,
ჯოყოლა როგორ არიო.
ვის ცოლი ვის ქმარსა სტირის?
რას სჩადის ჭკვაზე მცდარიო?!
იქნება ჰკლავენ ჯოყოლას,
სახლსაც შაუხსნეს კარიო!
წამოდგა, იხედებოდა,
როგორც დამთხვარი ნადირი,
ხედნებ-ხედნებით ამოვლო
ხევის კლდიანი ნაპირი;
წყვდიადში საზარლად ისმის
წყალთა ანაძრახი საყვირი.
ამოვლო კრძალვით საფლავთან,
მკვდარსა მუხლ-მოყრით დაეყრდნო,
ქვითინებს გულამოსკვნითა,
ცრემლსა სიპ ქვა დაედნო,
აიხსნა დანა, მიჰმართა
ზვიადაურსა იმითა,
ააჭრა ნიშნად, სახსოვრად
სამი ბალანი პირითა,
ჩიქილის ტოტში შეხვია
ბროლის თითებით თლილითა...
ეს რა ხმა ესმის, დგანდგარი?
ყურებს გაუდის ჟივილი...
საფლავებიდან მოესმის
მკვდარების წყრომა და ჩივილი!
თითქოს ბალღებიც ატირდენ,
გაუდისთ მწარედ წივილი!

81

She is waiting for dark, so she
Can weep for the dead by night;
She gave barely a thought
To her Jokhala,
A wife is mourning another's man
What is the madwoman doing?
Perhaps they are killing Jokhala,
Breaking down the doors of the house!
She rose and glanced around
A frightened creature;
Swiftly she climbed
The mountainous cliffs;
With the fearful noise of the waters
Hissing in the gloom.
She climbed to the grave, leaned
There, then knelt in reverence,
She was sobbing, out of breath;
Tears melted the stone.
She took a knife and approached
Zviadauri's corpse,
She cut three hairs from his beard
For a keepsake,
She wrapped them round a coarse twig
With her tapering sculpted fingers.
What is that deafening noise?
Her ears are ringing...
From the graves can be heard
The anger and moans of the dead!
As if infants were crying too,
Wailing bitterly!

საერთო წყრომის ხმა ისმის,
საერთო გულის ტკივილი:
"რას შვრება უნამუსოვო",
გამწარებულნი ჩიოდენ, -
"მადალი ღმერთი გრისხავდეს!"
სამართით შემოჰკიოდენ.
აჩქარებული ღრუბლები
ცის პირზე გადმოდიოდენ.
გაიქცა, მირბის, იხედავს, -
მკვდარნი მისდევენ, სწორია.
"შინით საღ გაგვეხვეწები,
აქით თუ გაგვეშორია!?" ხმა ისმის დანადევნები,
მასვე იმახის გორია,
გარშემო დაყუდებული
განა ერთი და ორია.
"უნამუსოვო"! მისძახდენ
ტანდაწკეპილნი დეკანი,
ბალახნი, ქვანი, ქვიშანი,
იმ არე-მარეს მდებარნი.
აგერ, საფლავით ამოდგა
მისი მკვდარი ძმა ებარი,
თავის ტოლებში უსწორო,
ქისტეთს გათქმული მხედარი.
თან მიჰკიოდა თავის დას,
სიტყვა პირს მოსდის მჭეხარი:
"ვაჰ, დაო, დაო, რა მიყავ?
რისხვა რად დამეც მედგარი?
მეორეს საფლავში ჩამდევ,
ერთს სამარეში მდებარი!
მაგით მიმტკიცებ დობასა,

It's the voice of a shared anger,
Of a common grief:
'What are you doing, you shameful wretch'
Was their bitter complaint,
'Almighty God will vent his anger on you!'
Was the cry from the grave.
Swift clouds
Appeared on the surface of the sky…
She ran away, looking back,
The dead themselves ran after her,
'Where can you hide yourself,
If you try to escape us now?'
The voices behind her cry,
The mountains echo their words,
Reverberating everywhere
Not just in one place or two.
'Traitor!' they all cry,
The peerless stallions,
The grasses, stones, and sand,
All around.
Here, from his grave, rises
Her dead brother, Ebari,
Unequalled among his peers,
Famed horseman of the Kists;
He shouted after his sister,
With thunderous words:
'Oh, my sister, what have you done to me?
Why do you shame me so?
You have dug me a second grave,
Though I am dead and buried!
Is this how you prove yourself my sister,

შენი ქალობა ეგ არი?!"
ბილიკზე მოსუნსულებდა
სასაფლაოსკე მყეფარი.

VIII
- სად მიხვალ, სადა, წყეულო?
საითკე მიეჩქარები?!
ვინ გაჭმევს კაის ყმის ლეშსა?
ძაღლო, დაგიდგა თვალები!
შენს საჯიჯგნადაც გამხდარა
ზვიადაურის ძვალები!? -
სთქვა ეს აღაზამ და ქვეჰსა
ესროდა ხშირა-ხშირადა.
მირბის და მისდევს შმაგადა
კლდიანის ხევის პირადა.
ხმა ისევ ესმის მკვდრებისა,
მას ბანს აძლევენ მთანიცა,
სამდურავს ეუბნებიან
აღაზას გიშრის თმანიცა.
მოუახლოვდა თავის სახლს,
სინათლე მოსჩანს იქითა;
უნდა იძახოს: "მიშველეთ",
ხმა მიაწვდინოს შიგითა.
მაგრამ ვერ ამბობს ვერაფერს,
ოფლი წყლად მოსდის შუბლზედა.
მივიდა სულშეხუთული
და გადაიქცა ზღუბლზედა.
კერის პირს იწდა ჯოყოლა,
მუხლი გადეგდო მუხლზედა.
"ვაჰმეო," - ეს კი იძახა,

Is this your womanhood?'
He glided along the path,
He howled towards the graveyard.

VIII

(Aghaza) 'What are you after, damn you?
Where are you going?
Who permits you to tear at a good man's flesh?
You dog, with greedy eyes!
Are Zviadauri's bones
For you to pick at?'
So Aghaza cried,
Hurling a shower of stones.
The dead run behind her menacingly,
Along the edge of the rocky ravine.
She can still hear their voices,
Echoed by the mountains.
Aghaza's agate black hair
Was filled with their disapproval.
As she neared her house,
She saw light streaming from it;
She wanted to scream for help,
Wanted her voice to be heard,
But she couldn't speak a word,
Sweat poured from her forehead...
She felt she was suffocating,
Poured out like water on the threshold.
Jokhala was seated by the hearth,
One knee crossed over the other,
'Woe is me,' she said, that's all,

სიტყვა გაუშრა ენაზე.
ქმარმა მოჰხვია ცოლს ხელი
და მიათრია კერაზე.
- რა დაგემართა, დიაცო? -
ჩაეკითხება მშფოთარე, -
სხვა სადარდელი მაქლია,
ახლა შენ მექმნა მოზარე?!
რა დაგემართა, რა არი?
მითხარ, გახსენი ბაგეო!
ხომ არვინ მოიწადინა
გადაეგორე მკლავზეო?
მითხარ, არ გაჭმევ იმის ჯავრს,
ვანანებ ემავ წამზეო.
ჩემის ნამუსის შემბღალავს
მალე მოვიყვან ჭკვაზეო,
როგორც ვანანე მუსასა
მიხდომა სხვისა კარზეო. -
პასუხს ელოდა ცოლისგან,
დასჩერებოდა თავზეო.
და თანაც ხანჯარს ჰბღუჯავდა,
ხელი ეკიდა ტარზეო.
ქალი ვერაფერს ამბობდა,
გაჰმტკნარებოდა სახეო.
თავს დასტრიალებს ჯოყოლა,
ელის, რას ეტყვის ცოლია,
შუადამის დროს აღაზამ
თანთან მოიცა გონია.
უთხრა ჯოყოლას: - "რას ამბობ?
თავი რად დაიღონია?
რად მოიგონებ იმასა,

The words died on her tongue.
The husband embraced his wife,
And helped her to the hearth.
'What has happened to you, woman?'
He asked, anxiously.
As if I lacked for sorrows,
Have you become one too?
What's happened, what is it?
Tell me, open your lips!
Has anyone tried
To grasp you in his arms?
Tell me. I'll not be angry
I'll make him regret in an instant
Any disrespect to my honour,
I'll knock the foolishness out of him,
As I made Musa regret
Coming to our door.'
He was waiting for an answer,
Standing over her,
At the same time gripping his dagger,
His hand on the hilt.
The woman could not speak,
Though her face looked calm.
Jokhala walked all round her,
Waiting for what she might say.
By midnight, Aghaza
Had slowly come to her senses.
She said to Jokhala: 'What is all this?
Why are you so troubled?
Why do you imagine
What has no reality?

რაიც არ მოსაგონია?
სულ ტყუილია... კაცისა
არსად მინახავს ჭაჭანი,
ვინ გამიბედავს მაგასა,
რად მინდა ლეჩაქ კაბანი?!
სასაფლაოდამ დავბრუნდი,
შენს ცხენს ვეძებდი ხევებში,
ცხენის მაგივრად ბედკრული
შიგ შევვერიე დევებში.
დამიხვდა შავ-ნაბდიანი,
უზარმაზარის ტანისა,
ჯერაც თვალებში მიელავს
სიმყრალე იმის კანისა;
დიდ-ყურა, კბილებ-დაჯუნა,
უმსგავსო, ფერად შავისა;
ხელები გამომიწვადა,
დიდი ხელები თავისა,
მთის ოდნად სჩანდა მის თავზე
მოშავფრო ქუდი ტყავისა.
თან მითხრა: ჩემთან წამოდი,
ჩემთან იცხოვრე, ქალაო,
ზევრი მაქვს ოქრო და ვერცხლი,
არაფერს დაგიმალაო.
მე გამოვიქე, შევშინდი,
დევიც მომდევდა ღრიალით;
მთელი ქვეყანა იძროდა
იმის ფეხების ქვეშ გრიალით;
მზარავდა ეს ხმაც, მთა-ბარიც
წაღმა-უკუღმა ტრიალით,
ძლივს მოვაღწიე და გამცნე

It's all illusion...a man?
I've not seen a living soul.
Who would dare do that to me?
Don't I wear a bride's head-scarf?
I returned from the graveyard
I was searching for your horse in the ravine
Instead of a horse, alas
I met with giants.
One dressed in a black felt cloak,
With an enormous body:
(Lightning in my eyes,
The reek of its flesh)
With vast ears, and teeth,
Loathsome, and black in colour.
He reached out his hands,
His enormous hands,
On his head like a mountain-top
Was a dark hat of leather,
He said: "Come with me,
Live with me, woman,
I have a heap of gold and silver
I'll hide nothing from you."
I ran in fear from him,
The giant too was running and howling,
The earth was shaking
Under his lumbering feet;
The voice scared me, the mountains
And valleys too,
Winding this way and that,
I barely reached here to tell you,

ჩემი ვაება ხრიალით".
ჯოყოლა ეტყვის: დევს გარდა
სხვა რამ საქმეა კიდევა,
ჩემს ჭკვას არ სჯერა ნათქვამი,
ჩემი ფიქრები ირევა.
ნამტირალევი რადა ხარ?
დაწვებზე ცრემლი გდენია;
ჩქარა სთქვი, სწორედ მითხარი,
თორემ ვერ მომითმენია!
სადარდო, საგულისხმო რამ
გრძნობა გულს გადაგფრენია.
ჩემს თვალებს ვერ დაემალვის
იმ გრძნობის ნაკვალევია;
არ შაიძლება არ დაჩნდეს
ნასვამი, დანალევია!..
- რა დაგიმალო, ჯოყოლავ,
ან რად შემრისხავ თქმისადა? -
ეტყოდა ცოლი და ნაზი
თრთოლა მიეცა ხმისადა: -
ცრემლები შემიწირია
იმ შენის მეგობრისადა.
ძლიერ შემბრალდა ბეჩავი,
რომ უცხოეთში კვდებოდა,
არც ნათესავი, არც მომმე,
რომ ვისმე შეჰბრალებოდა!
მაგრამ, როს ჰკლავდენ ხანჯრითა,
ოდნავაც არა ჰკრთებოდა.
იქნებ შენც გცოდე, ღმერთსაცა,
მაგრამ ვიტირე, რა ვქნაო!..
-

91

Out of breath and suffering.
Jokhala said: 'Besides this giant,
There must have been something else,
I can't believe what you say,
My thoughts are confused.
Why were you crying?
Tears have flowed down your cheeks;
Tell me now, tell me truthfully,
Or I'll lose patience!
Some sorrow, some vital
Feeling has pierced your heart.
You can't hide from my eyes
Every trace of that feeling;
There is no way to erase
Every trace of drink from the cup!...'
'Why should I hide it from you, Jokhala,
What in my words could enrage you?'
The wife said, tremulous
Quivering in her voice,
'I sacrificed my tears
To that guest of yours.
I felt pity for that unfortunate man
Dying here in a foreign place,
With no kin, no brother by,
To feel pity for him!
Who when he was struck by the sword,
Never even flinched.
Perhaps I sinned against you, and God,
Yet I cried for him, what could I do!...'

მაგისთვის როგორ შეგრისხავ?
ტყუილს სჯობს სიმართლის თქმაო.
იტირე?! მადლი გიქნია,
მე რა გამგე ვარ მაგისა?
დიაცს მუდამაც უხდება
გლოვა ვაჟკაცის კარგისა.

IX

მეორეს დილას ალაზამ
ძროხა გარეკა მთისაკე,
ჩამოდიოდენ ფრინვლები,
იზიდებოდენ მკვდრისაკე;
ალაზაც მიიპარება
სასაფლაოს თავს კლდისაკე.
იქიდამ აფრთხობს ყორნებსა,
სვავთა მხარ-მოფარფაშეთა,
ორბებსა გაუმაძღრებსა,
მკვდრის ლეშზე მოყაშყაშეთა;
ხელს ამუშავებს და ჰმალავს
თვალებს, მზებრ მოკაშკაშეთა.
კლდიდამ გადისვრის კენჭებსა
და თან წინდას ქსოვს ვითომა,
ოსტატობს, ხალხმა ვერ შესძლოს
იმის ფიქრების მიხდომა.

X

ბისოს მოვიდა ამბავი,
ვით ნაქუხარი მეხადა:
"მოუკლავთ ზვიადაური,
ცით ჩამოსული სვეტადა,

'Why would I be angered at that?
To speak truth is better than lying.
You shed tears? You have shown mercy!
Who am I to judge that a wrong?
It is always fitting a woman
Should mourn a brave man.'

IX

Next morning, Aghaza
Drives out the cattle,
Birds are swooping,
Attracted by the corpse;
Aghaza too is drawn
To the rocky heights of the graveyard,
From which she scares the ravens,
The vultures, wings beating,
The insatiable eagles,
Feasting on the spoils of the dead;
With furtive movements of her hand,
Her eyes glittering like the sun,
She throws pebbles from the rocks,
While seeming to be knitting,
So cleverly, that no one
Can guess at her thoughts.

X

News reached Biso,
Like a clap of thunder:
'They have killed Zviadauri,
One like sunlight from the sky,

ფშავ-ხევსურეთის ფარ-ხმალი,
გამოსადეგი მეტადა!”
შავის ამბისა გამგონეთ
ზარი გამართეს დედათა.
ბისოს ტიროდა ზებერი,
მოსთქვამს, ქვითინებს მწარედა:
”ზედკრული რად ვარ ცოცხალი?
მეც მიწას მიმაბარეთა;
მკლავნი მაჩვენეთ შვილისა,
მოიტათ, ჩამაბარეთა!
ჩემის შვილისა მარჯვენით
გულს მიწა მომაყარეთა;
ვაჰმე, რადა ვარ ცოცხალი?
რისთვის-და ვსთელავ არეთა?!
მკვდარნო, რად არ მეც ადრევე
თქვენთან არ დამიბარეთა?
როგორ ვიგონო თავის ძე
ურჯულოს არე-მარეთა?!”
ვაჟკაცთო გაიგეს ამბავი,
გასაგონარი ჭირითა,
ერთმანეთს გადაექრახნენ
ბოღმით შემკულის პირითა:
რად გიკვირთ, როცა ჩვენს მფარველს
ცხარის ცრემლითა ვსტირითა?!
გამოიტანეს შუბები
დუმით ნაპოხის ცხვირითა,
ფარ-ხმალით მოკაზმულები
ჯარს ამზადებენ დილითა.
ეს ხომ ახალი არ არის,
სისხლმა იდინოს მილითა.

The shield and sword of Pshav-Khevsureti,
Our vital defence!'
Those hearing the black news
The women, gathered;
In Biso his aged mother is crying,
Lamenting, sobbing bitterly,
'Oh, why am I still alive?
Bury me too in the earth!
Show me my son's limbs,
Bring him, let me touch them!
With my son's right hand
Throw earth on my heart!
Oh, why am I still living?
Why am I still treading the earth?
Oh, why have the dead, failed
To order me to their realm?
How can I, remain
On sacrilegious soil?
Brave men heard the news,
Heard it in sorrow,
Grappled with each other
Grieved, roused by anger…
Hardly surprising; their defender
They now mourned with bitter tears!
They brandished spears,
Sharpened and greased the blades,
Donned shields and swords,
Gathered their forces for the morning.
Nothing strange indeed
If blood flows in torrents.

იმახის აპარეკაი:
"საგძალი გინდათ კვირისა!"
"ქუდზე კაც უნდა წავიდეს!" -
ბაბურაული ჰყვირისა.
აღელვებულთა ბორგვნაა,
ხმა არ გეგონსთ სტვირისა!

XI
- კარში გამოდი, ჯოყოლავ,
წყნარად ნუ სწევხარ კერასა,
რამდენი ხალხი მოერტყა
იმ ჩვენის მთების წვერასა!
ჩვენთან მოდიან სტუმრადა,
ჩვენ გვიპიროზენ წვევასა.
შეგვანანეზენ დედათა
შვილთა აკვნების რწევასა.
საქონელს ერეკეზიან,
რეულოზაა როგორი?!
აავსო ჯარმა, გაჰხედე,
ჯარეგის თავი, სამ-გორი,
დამთხვალთა მენახირეთა
კლდეები მოსდევს ნაგორი.
წადი, უშველე თავისებს,
მტრის დასახვედრად მირზიან,
შენც ისე წადი, ჯოყოლავ,
როგორაც სხვანი მიდიან.
- გავყვე?! რას ამბობ, ჭკვა-თხელო?
არ გამივლევენ ახლოსა!
მარტოკამ უნდა ვიომო,
მთელმა ჯარეგამ მნახოსა;

97

Apareka cried:
You'll need rations for a week!'
'A man from every clan!'
Babarauli yelled.
It was the din of men roused for battle,
Not the music of the flute!

XI

'Run outside, Jokhala,
Don't lie there calmly by the hearth,
See the force that has reached
Our mountain heights!
They are coming to visit,
They will soon be our guests,
They will make our women
Rue their rocking of the cradle,
They are driving off the cattle,
What is all this confusion!
See, their army has seized
The heights of Jaregi, and Samgori,
The wastelands of the shepherds,
They are descending from the cliffs.
Go, help your kin,
They're advancing on the enemy,
Go too, Jokhala,
Go with all the others.'
'Follow them? What are you saying, fool?
They won't let me near them!
I'll have to fight alone,
Let all Jarega see it;

ვინ ერთგულია, ვინ არა,
ქვეყანამ დაინახოსა.
ქისტებს ორგული ვგონივარ,
გამდგარი თავის რჯულზედა,
ჰფიქრობენ, ვითომ ჯოყოლამ
თავი გაჰყიდა ფულზედა,
ქისტეთის მოღალატე ვარ,
ხელაღებული სულზედა;
მოაქვთ და ცოცხალს მადებენ
საფლავის ქვასა გულზედა.
ამას ამბობდა ჯოყოლა,
თან აჯჯარს ისხამს ტანზედა:
წელზე შაიბა ფრანგული,
თოფი გადიგდო მხარზედა,
ქისტს არ მაუდის ჯიშადა
მუზარადის დგმა თავზედა.
მარტოკა მიდის ცალს მხარეს,
თავდადებული ცდაზედა,
მტრის დასახვედრად სხვანიცა
შამოეფინნენ მთაზედა.

XII
ჩამოდის ხევსურთა ჯარი
დროშა მოჰქონდა წინასა;
მიჰმართეს სასაფლაოსა,
მდუმარეს ქისტთა ზინასა:
მოქებნონ თავისი მკვდარი,
მოკრიბონ გმირის ძვალები,
ზვიადაურის მტანჯველთა
ძირში მოსთხარონ თვალები.

Who is loyal, who is not,
Let the country see it.
The Kists think I'm a traitor,
Renouncing my own cult,
They think Jokhala,
Has sold himself for gain,
That I've betrayed Kisteti,
One careless of his own soul;
They are bringing a gravestone
To set on my living heart.'
As Jokhala spoke,
He was donning his body-armour:
Strapping his sword to his waist,
Slinging his gun from his shoulder,
It is not a Kist tradition
To wear a helmet on the head.
He walks along by himself,
Intent on meeting
With the foe.
The Kists are scattered over the heights.

XII

The army of the Khevsurs advances,
Their flag-bearer in the lead;
They swarm towards the graveyard,
The Kists' house of silence:
They seek their dead warrior,
To gather his bones,
To put out the eyes
Of Zviadauri's tormentors.

დაუხვდათ ქისტის ჯარიცა,
ხევ-ხევის პირას მალუღი;
შამოესროლეს თოფები,
მაჭრები შემოსალტული;
გზას არ უთმობენ ხევსურთა
ბიჭები ამოსხარტული.
ორივე მხრიდამ თოფებსა
ზედ დაკიჯინით ისვრიან,
ორსავე საქმე აწუხებს,
ორნივე მედგრად იბრძვიან.
ბლომად დალია ტყვიამა
სისხლი, - მომოვა ქუჩია,
მაინც არ გატყდენ ქისტები,
სდგანან ვით ციხე-ბურჯია.
ბაბურაულმა ხევსურთა
ხმალ-და-ხმალ ჩასვლა ურჩია.
მივიდა საქმე ხმალზედა,
ფარმა გზა მისცა საკაფი,
საძევარი აქვთ ხევსურთა
ძვირი განძი და ალაფი.
ფარო, ნუ ჰმტყუვნობ გორდასა,
შენა ხარ მაგის ჯალაფი;
თავქვე მორბინალთ ხევსურთა
წინ კლდეე დაუხვდათ წარაფი.
კლდიდამ გადუხტა უეცრად
ქისტი ხმალ-მოღერებითა,
აკვირვებს ქისტის ლაშქარსა
მტრის ჯარის მოგერებითა.
ზოგს მოტყუება ეგონა,
ამზობდენ მოჩვენებითა:

But they were met by the Kists,
Concealed at the gully's edge;
Who grasp their guns,
They won't yield
To the Khevsurs.
Agile young men
On both sides fire their guns
Shouting their battle cries,
Both sides suffer wounds,
Both sides fight on, regardless.
The bullets had their fill
Of blood, harming many.
Still the Kists did not break,
They stood firm as a fortress.
Babarauli of the Khevsurs,
Called for a sabre attack.
It came down to cold steel,
Shields gave way to sabres.
The Khevsurs are seeking
Rich treasure and spoils;
Shield, do not despise the sword
That hangs beside you.
The Khevsurs scrambling down
Met an insurmountable boulder.
Suddenly from behind it,
Sprang a lone Kist with a sabre,
Astounding the army of Kists,
By repulsing the enemy force.
Some thought it a mirage,
They called out, in disbelief,

- ეგ ვინ უხვდება ხევსურთა?
ჩვენი მხარეა, ვინ არი?
- ეგ უნდა ჯოყოლა იყოს,
სწორედ, ნამდვილად ის არი! -
სთქვა ერთმა, სხვანიც დასთანხმდენ,
გაოცებულნი უცქერენ.
როგორ არ უფთხის გროვასა,
თუმცა ხმალ-ხანჯრებს უდერენ.
მოჰკლეს კიდეცა, იქცევა,
მკერდს ხანჯრის წვერით უწერენ.
ქისტთ გაუხარდათ დიაღაც, -
"მოჰკლან, თუ მოჰკლეს - ახია!
ეხლაც მასხარად აგვიგდო,
წინად ხომ ბევრჯელ აგვრია,
სოფლისა გადრა ინდომა,
ჩვენ-კი ტალახში გაგვრია.
მარტოკა მტრის ჯარს დაუხვდა,
სწორედ დავლათით დაგვრია."
ხევსურთ ჯოყოლა გაწირეს
მკვდარი, კლდის თავსა, კეტამზე.
თითონ დაესხნენ ქისტებსა,
ჩამოეფინნენ ფერდაზე.
გახდა ხმალ-ხანჯრის ტრიალი,
დაკრული მიდის მკერდამდე;
ფარ-ხმალის ჩხერა, წკრიალი
ცას ადიოდა ღმერთამდე.
გაიქცა ქისტის ლაშქარი,
კოშკებს მიჰმართა გრიალით,
უკან მისდევენ ხევსურნი,
თავზე ჩაჩქნების პრიალით;

'Who is attacking the Khevsurs?
Is it one of us? Who is he?'
'It looks like Jokhala,
Yes it's him indeed!'
One shouted, others agreed,
They all stared, dumbfounded.
At his disdain for the enemy force,
Though they brandish swords and daggers.
Then the enemy killed him,
Pierced his chest with their sabre tips.
At that the Kists too rejoiced:
'Let them kill him, he deserves to die!
Even now he treats us like fools,
As he has spurned us before,
Daring to set himself over all the rest,
And cover us in shame.
He met the enemy army alone,
And won over us by chance.'
The Khevsurs slaughtered Jokhala
On the rocky summit, on the heights.
They attacked the Kists,
Scattered over the slope.
A whirl of daggers and sabres,
Struck them in their chests;
The ringing and clatter of shield and sword
Rose to God above.
The Kist army fled,
They went scurrying towards their towers,
The Khevsurs chasing after,
Their helms glittering;

მოკრიბეს სასაფლაოზე
ზვიადას ძვლები ტრიალით:
ზოგი სად ეგდო, ზოგი სად,
ფრინველთ ნაჯიჯგნი ფრიალით.
მოკრიბეს ძვლები ხურჯინში
და გამობრუნდენ შინათვე,
ასრულეს გულის წადილი,
დანაპირები წინათვე.
გამოირეკეს ცხვარ-ძროხა,
გადმოავლიეს მთანია;
ამოიყარეს მტრის ჯავრი,
სადარდო რაღა არია?!
უცხოეთს მაინც არ დაჰრჩათ,
შინ მოაქვთ თავის მკვდარია,
ფშავ-ხევსურეთის იმედი,
ქავ-ციხე, რკინის კარია.
მომმენი დაიტირებენ
თავის მკვდარს თავის წესზედა,
მიაბარებენ სამარეს
მამა-პაპათა გვერდზედა:
ძვირად ღირს დანადინარი
თავისის ცრემლი მკერდზედა!

XIII
- უცხოს კაცისა მოზარევ,
ხევსურთ მოგიკლეს ქმარია.
წადი, იტირე, აღაზავ,
სამარეს მიაბარია.
თავს დაჰყრანტალებს ყორანი,
წვერ-ულვაშს უცრის ქარია.

They gathered from the graveyard
The bones of Zviadauri:
Scattered some here, some there,
Torn apart by carrion birds.
They put the bones in their saddle-bags,
And headed for home,
Their hearts' desire achieved,
The vengeance they had sworn.
They gathered the sheep and cattle,
Drove them over the mountains;
They took revenge on their foes,
Answering every desire!
His bones they carried with them,
Home from that foreign soil,
The Hope of Pshav-Khevsureti,
Their Fortress, their Iron Door.
His brothers will cry for him,
For the dead, according to custom,
They'll inter his bones to lie
Beside his ancestors:
The tears that ran down his chest,
Have exacted the highest price!

XIII

'Mourner of a stranger,
Khevsurs slew your husband.
Go mourn him, Aghaza,
Bury him in his grave.
The raven croaks at his head,
The wind sifts through his beard,

- შენს მტერსა ისეთი ყოფნა,
რო ჩემი ყოფნა მწარია!
აღარვინ მივლის ახლოსა,
არვინ მიჯირა მხარია.
იქვე დავმარხე კლდის თავზე,
საფლავიც გავუთხარია;
სუყველამ ზურგი მაქცია,
ყველაყა განწზე მდგარია.
სასაფლაოც კი შემიკრეს,
რო დამემარხა ცხედარი:
ჯოყოლამ გვიდალატაო,
მაგის ადგილი ეგ არი,
საცა მარტოკა ომობდა,
ჩვენთვისა ჩირქის მცხებარი,
თემის პირისა გამტეხი,
ორგული, დაუდეგარი.
ცეცხლი მწვავს, ძმაო, ცეცხლი მწვავს
უალო, მოუდებარი;
გულს მიკლავს, გონებას მირევს
ფიქრები გაუგებარი!
ცოლი სტიროდა ჯოყოლას,
ცრემლს ასხურებდა ხშირადა,
არჩვი ყელ-გადააგდებული,
თმა-ხშირი, მთვარე პირადა,
ეკერებოდა გულ-მკერდზე
ქმარს მარგალიტის ღილადა.

XIV
ღამეა ბნელი, დელგმაა,
დგანდგნარებს არე-მარეო.

(Aghaza): 'May your enemies know
The bitterness of my bitter existence!
Nobody comes near me,
Nobody cares about me.
I buried him on top of the cliff,
And I dug his grave myself.
All turn their backs on me,
All stand aside.
They even shut the graveyard,
Where I might bury my dead.'
'Jokhala betrayed us,
That is the place for him,
Where he fought alone,
Spreader of poison amongst us,
Destroyer of our health,
Traitorous, unrelenting.'
'Fire is burning me, brothers, fire is burning me,
Flameless, unmoving;
It slays my heart, confuses my mind,
With unfathomable thoughts!'
So the wife mourned Jokhala,
Shedding endless tears,
A chamois, with neck bent gracefully,
Loose hair, face like the moon,
She was sewing herself, like a pearl button,
To her husband's chest.

XIV

The night is dark, rain pours,
The ground is quivering.

ღმერთო, მოჰხედე ტანჯულთა,
უშველე, შაიწყალეო!
კარგი კარგია მაინცა, -
ბეჩავი შაიყვარეო!
ტანჯულთა ლოცვა-მუდარა
გულს ვარდად დაიყარეო!
თუ არ უშველი, საწყლების
სულები მიიბარეო!..
გეყო მაგდენი მუქარა,
ღრუბელო, გადიყარეო!
მდინარე მოჰქუხს, მრისხანებს,
ზედ ასქდებოდა ლოდებსა,
დღესაც ისევე ბოროტობს,
არ იცის, რისთვის ჰგოდებსა.
არ ეშინიან ტანჯვისა,
იმან არ იცის სიკვდილი.
ერთი რამ იცის მხოლოდა:
ცრემლის ღვრა, მაღლა ყვირილი,
მუდამ ჟამს უცინარობა,
მარტო ტირილი, ტირილი...
ქარი სცემს, დაბლა ხევებით
ჩამოკიჟინებს მთებითა;
ქალი სდგას, მდინარეს დასცქერს,
კლდეზე, გაშლილის თმებითა;
სხივ მიხდილს ვარსკვლავს მაგონებს
მკრთალად მთრთოლარის ყბებითა.
არ იღებს ხმასა... შემკრთალი
ჰკრთის, რომ დასცქერის მდინარეს;
რა საზარლადა ხმაურობს,
როგორ საზარლად მდინარებს!

God, take care of those in torment,
Help them, have mercy on them!
Good is good despite all,
Show love to the wretched one!
Take the prayers of the tormented
To your heart like roses!
If you can't help, accept
The souls of those in pain!...
Enough of this threatening sky
Dissipate, you clouds!
The river thunders, angrily,
Bursting over the boulders,
It's wrath unchanged today,
Not knowing why it laments.
It has no fear of torment,
It knows nothing of death.
It only knows one thing:
Shedding its tears, and howling,
Endlessly joyless,
Forever howling and crying…
The wind scours the ravines
Shouting from the mountain;
On the cliff, the woman, her hair unbound
Stands, gazing at the river.
She seems like a fading star,
In the gloom her trembling mouth.
Speaks not a word…
She quivers, she stares at the river;
Dreadful the noise it makes,
Dreadful the way it flows!

ლაშ-დაღრენილი, სასტიკი
შავი ხეობა მძვინვარებს.
"თავს ნუ იკლავო!" აბა, თუ
ერთმა ურჩიოს მაინცა.
დახუჭა ქალმა თვალები,
მსწრაფლად მორევში ჩაიქცა.
- რაღად ვიცოცხლო, რიდასთვის?
ამას ჰფიქრობდა ქალია. -
ქისტეთში ჩემი ერთგული
კენჭიც კი არსად არია.
ორთავ შევცვდეთ ქისტებსა,
მათ შამიჩვენეს ქმარია...
მე უფრო დიდი ცოდვა მაქვს,
უცხოსთვის ცრემლი ვღვარია.
წაიღო წყალმა აღაზა,
ლამსა და ქვიშას შაჰრია.

XV
იმ კლდის თავს, საცა ჯოყოლა
მოჰკლეს ხევსურთა ბრძოლაში,
ღამ-ღამ ჰხედავენ სურათსა
ზვავისგან ნაგალს გორაში:
კლდის თავს წადგება ჯოყოლა,
სასაფლაოსკე იმახებს:
"ზვიადაურო, ძმობილო,
რად არ მაჩვენებ შენს სახეს?!"
სასაფლაოდამ წამოვა
აჩრდილი ფარ-ხმალიანი,
გულზე უწყვია დაკრეფით

Snarling, severe,
The black torrent rages.
'Do not drown yourself!'
If they would only call to her.
The woman shut her eyes,
Leapt swiftly into the depths.
'Why live on, to what end?
Such were her last thoughts.
In Kisteti no one cares for me,
Not one thing, not even a pebble.
Both of us harmed the Kists,
They damned my husband...
I bear a greater sin,
I shed tears for a stranger.'
The water took Aghaza,
Drowned her in its silt and sand.

XV

On that cliff-top, where Jokhala
Was slain in the fight with the Khevsurs,
At night they see an image,
Carved on the hill, by an avalanche:
Jokhala stands high on the boulder,
Shouting towards the graveyard:
'Zviadaur, my brother,
Why won't you show your face?'
From the graveyard there comes
A ghost with sword and shield,
He has crossed his arms

მკლავები სამკლავიანი.
მივა და მიესალმება
თავის ძმობილსა მდუმარედ.
იქვე ადაზაც ამოდის
სახე მოწყენით, მწუხარედ.
ენთება ცეცხლი მათს გვერდით,
მკრთალადა ბჟუტავს მთაზედა;
იმათ ჰმასპინძლობს ადაზა,
ჯიხვის მწვადს უწვავს ალზედა.
ვაჟკაცობისას ამბობენ,
ერთურთის დანდობისასა,
სტუმარ-მასპინძლის წესზედა
ცნობის და და-ძმობისასა.
როცა მათ ჰხედავს ერთადა
კაცი, ვერ ძღება ცქერითა;
მაგრამ გაჩნდება ჯანღი რამ
კურუმად შავის ფერითა,
დაეფარება სანახავს
წერა-მწერელის წერითა.
ზედ აწევს ჯადოსავითა,
არ დაიმტვრევა კვერითა,
ვერც შეულოცავს მლოცავი,
არც აიხდება ხელითა.
მხოლოდ მდინარის ხმა ისმის,
დაბლა მიქანავს ხველითა
და უფსკრულს დასცქერს პირიმზე
მოღერებულის ყელითა...

Over his heart,
He'll come and greet
His brother silently.
There Aghaza too will rise,
With a sad, mournful face.
A fire burns beside them,
Dimly smouldering on the mountain.
Aghaza plays host to her guests,
She roasts a ram over the flames.
They are drinking to courage,
To each others' respect
For the rites of host and guest,
To comradeship, brotherhood, sisterhood.
When you see them together
You can't have enough of gazing;
Yet something dark appears
Filling your sight,
Dense, black in colour,
As the words of the poet.
It shrouds it like an enchantment,
No weapon can pierce it,
No prayer can charm it away,
Nor any hand can remove it.
Only the river's noise is heard,
Raging downwards, roaring,
While beauty stares into its depths
Her neck bent, gracefully…

1893

ელეგია

მკრთალი ნათელი სავსე მთვარისა
მშობელს ქვეყანას ზედ მოჰფენოდა
და თეთრი ზოლი შორის მთებისა
ლაჟვარდ სივრცეში დაინთქმებოდა.

არსაიდამ ხმა არსით ძახილი!..
მშობელი შობილს არრას მეტყოდა,
ზოგჯერ კი ტანჯვით ამომახილი
ქართვლის ძილშია კვნესა ისმოდა.

ვიდექ მარტოკა და მთების ჩრდილი...
კვლავ ჩემს ქვეყნის ძილს ეალერსება.
ოხ, ღმერთო ჩემო! სულ ძილი, ძილი,
როსდა გვეღირსოს ჩვენ გაღვიძება?!.

Elegy by Ilia Chavchavadze

Translation by Lela Jgerenaia

dim light of a full moon
had fallen upon its native land
and the white stripe of the distant mountains
was being absorbed in the azure space.

from nowhere no voice, from nowhere no call!...
mother to an offspring, would tell me nothing,
and sometimes the torment crying
In the Georgian's sleep moaning was heard!

I was standing alone... and the shade of the mountains
caresses my country's sleep again.
oh, my god! always slumber, slumber,
when will we have earned awakening?!..

მე და ღამე

ეხლა როცა ამ სტრიქონს ვწერ, შუაღამე იწვის, ღნება,
სიო, სარკმლით მონაქროლი, ველთა ზღაპარს მეუბნება.
მთვარით ნაფენს არემარე ვერ იცილებს ვერცხლის საბანს,
სიო არხევს და ატოკებს ჩემს სარკმლის წინ იასამანს.

ცა მტრედისფერ, ლურჯ სვეტებით ისე არის დასერილი,
ისე არის სავსე გრძნობით, ვით რითმებით ეს წერილი.
საიდუმლო შუქით არე ისე არის შესუდრული,
ისე სავსე უხვ გრძნობებით, ვით ამ ღამეს ჩემი გული.

დიდი ხნიდან საიდუმლოს მეც ღრმად გულში დავატარებ,
არ ვუმჭდავნებ ქვეყნად არვის, ნიავსაც კი არ ვაკარებ.
რა იციან მეგობრებმა, თუ რა ნაღველს იტევს გული,
ან რა არის მის სიღრმეში საუკუნოდ შენახული.

ვერ მომპარავს ზნელ გულის ფიქრს წუთი წუთზე უამესი,
საიდუმლოს ვერ მომტაცებს ქალის ხვევნა და ალერსი.
ვერც ძილის დროს ნახი ოხვრა და ვერც თასი ღვინით სავსე,
ვერ წამართმევს, რაც გულის ზნელ სიღრმეში მოვათავსე.

მხოლოდ ღამემ, უძილობის დროს სარკმელში მოკამკამემ,
იცის ჩემი საიდუმლო, ყველა იცის თეთრმა ღამემ.
იცის – როგორ დავრჩი ობლად, როგორ ვევნე და ვეწამე,
ჩვენ ორნი ვართ ქვეყანაზე: მე და ღამე, მე და ღამე!

117

I and Night by Galaktion Tabidze

Translated by Lela Jgerenaia

Now, as I write this line, midnight continues to burn,
At the window, the breeze sighs: it tells me a tale of the fields.
The landscape spread by the moon, can't throw off itssilvery covers,
The breeze sighs, quivers and sways the lilac beyond the glass.

The sky slashed by columns of lilac and darkest blue
As filled with feelings, as my verse is with lines,
The region's shrouded in clandestine light,
As filled with sensation's flow, my heart in the night.

For ages I carry this secret, too, deep in my heart,
Hidden from all, not even touched by the breeze,
What do my friends know of my inner grief
Of what is preserved forever there in its deeps.

The loveliest moment can't steal the dark of my thoughts.
Woman's kiss and embrace can't possess my secret.
Neither soft moans while I sleep nor the bowl filled with wine
Can rob me of what I conceal in the depths of my heart.

Only night, in insomnia's transparent window
Knows this secret of mine, white night knows it all
Knows how I was left: bereft, hurt and tormented,
We are as one in this world, I...I and the night!

მძულხარ – მიყვარხარ

მძულხარ იმიტომ, უქლური რად ხარ
ძლიერი მკლავით, მტირალი სახით
და შენი ბედი, ბედი შავბედი
რად შემოსილა სულ მუდამ შავით?

მოკვეთის მგმობა და მტრის ვერ მწნობო,
შენ დამღუპავთან მისული ზავით,
ბედის მომლოდნევ გვერძე წოლითა,
ცარელ ჯიბით და ბნელის თავით.

მაინც მიყვარხარ, ჩემს წყლულს ოცნებას
ზედ აკერიხარ ალმასის ღილად;
ვერ დაგივიწყე, გულს არ ჰშორდები,
მღვიძარა ვარ, თუ მივიქცე ძილად.

სამსალა პირს მწვავს, გუნებას მირევს,
ბოლოს კი ისევ მეჩვენა ტკბილად.
ესეც წესია ალბათ ბუნების:
შენ დედა თუ ხარ, გეკუთვნი შვილად!

119

I Hate You - I Love You by Vazha-Pshavela

Translated by Lela Jgerenaia

I hate you because, why are you powerless
with strong arm and weeping face
and your fate, fate black fate
why shrouded always in black?

You who condemn the friend and fail to recognize the enemy,
you who conclude a truce with your undoer,
awaiting your fate by lying on your side,
with empty pocket and unlit mind.

Still I love you, onto my wounded dream
you are sewn like a diamond button;
I could never forget you, you're never apart from my heart,
whether I'm awake or asleep.

Poison burns my mouth, confusing my mood,
at the end it still seemed sweet.
Also most likely it's a law of nature;
If you are mother, I belong to you as child!

იას უთხარით ტურფასა

იას უთხარით ტურფასა
მოვა და შეგჩამს ჭიაო,
მაგრე მოხდენით, ლამაზო,
თავი რომ აგიღიაო!

შენ თუ გგონია სიცოცხლე
სამოთხის კარი ღიაო;
ნუ მოხვალ, მიწას ეფარე,
მოსვლაში არა ყრიაო.

ნუ ნახავს მზესა, ინანებს,
განა სულ მუდამ მზეაო!
მიწავ, შენ გებრალებოდეს
ეს ჩემი ტურფა იაო,
შენ უპატრონე, ემშობლე,
როგორაც შენი ზნეაო.

Tell the Beautiful Violet by Vazha-Pshavela

Translated by Lela Jgerenaia

Tell the lovely violet
A worm will come and eat you up,
'cause so elegantly, you beauty,
you've coyly raised your head!

If you think of life
as heaven's open door;
do not come up, seek shelter in the earth,
there's naught to come up for.

If she won't see the sun, she will regret,
as it isn't always sunny!
Earth, feel pity
for my lovely violet,
take care of her, mother her,
as is in your nature.

მემღერება და ვიმღერი

(სიმღერა)

-მემღერება და ვიმღერი,
გულზე მჭირს სამი იარა:
წარსულზე ფიქრი მაწუხებს,
აწმყოში არა ყრია რა
და მომავალის ფიქრებიც
არავინ გამიზიარა!

ნისლებში გახვეულია,
ოდნავა ბჟუტავს ვარსკვლავი,
ვეღარ ვაშორებ თვალებსა,
ერთხელ იმისი მნახავი.
დაჯინებულის მის ცქერით
შევიქენ დასაძრახავი.

გულში კი წყლული იზრდება,
სულსა მიხუთავს, მაღონებს,
სიკვდილი არა მშადიან,
თუმც ტანჯვა სიკვდილს მაგონებს,
და ჩემი ყოფნა ასეთი
საწყალს ამირანს მაგონებს.

ხმალიც გვერდს უძე, გოშიაც
ერთგულად აღრღნის რკინასა;
არც ხმალი მოდის გმირთანა,
ვერც თითონ სწვდება იმასა.
გაღრღნილი ჯაჭვიც მთელია,
ჰხედავს მეორე დილასა;

სწვავს ტანჯვა-ვაების ცეცხლი
პატრონს და იმის ფინასა:
მომავლის სხივი აქარვებს
გმირის ოხვრას და გმინვას.

I Feel Like Singing and I Sing by Vazha-Pshavela

(A song)

Translated by Lela Jgerenaia

I feel like singing and I sing,-
I have three wounds on my heart:
thinking about the past troubles me,
There's nothing given in the present
and thoughts of the future
no one has shared with me!

wrapped in mists,
the star barely flickers,
I can't take my eyes off it,
seeing it once.
persisting in watching it
I became culpable.

but in the heart the ulcer grows,
chokes my soul, grieves me,
I don't desire death,
although torture reminds me of death,
and my being that way
reminds me of poor Amirani.

the sword lies next to him, the dog too
devotedly gnawing iron;
the sword does not come to the hero,
nor is he able to reach it himself,
the gnawed chain is also intact,
he sees the next morning;

torturing fire burns
the master and his dog:
the future's ray of hope dispels
the hero's moans and groans.

რამ შემქმნა ადამიანად?

რამ შემქმნა ადამიანად?
რატომ არ მოვედ წვიმადა,
რომ მყოფილიყავ მუდამა
ღრუბელთ გულ-მკერდის მდივადა,
მიწაზე გადმოსაგდებად
ცვარად ან თოვლად ცივადა?
არ გამწირავდა პატრონი
ასე ოხრად და ტიელადა!
ცაშივე ამიტაცებდა,
თან მატარებდა შვილადა.
ასე არ დამჩირდებოდა
სულ მუდამ ყოფნა ფრთხილადა.
მზის მოტრფიალე ვივლიდი
სიკვდილის გამაწზილადა;
მაღლა ცა, დაბლა ხმელეთი
მე მექნებოდა წილადა.
გავიხარებდი მთა-ბარსა
ოდეს ვნახავდი მწვანედა,
მორწყულსა ჩემის ოფლითა,
ყვავილებს შიგნით, გარეთა.
გადავუშლიდი გულმკერდსა
დღისით მზეს, ღამით მთვარესა.
სიცოცხლეს ვაგრძნობინებდი
მომაკვდავ არემარესა.
თოვლად ქცეულსა გულშია
ცეცხლად იმედი მრჩებოდა,
რომ ისევ ჩემი სიკვდილი
სიცოცხლედ გადიკცეოდა
და განახლებულ ბუნებას
ყელ-ყურზე მოეხვეოდა.

Why Was I Created as a Human? by Vazha-Pshavela

Translated by Lela Jgerenaia

Why was I made as a human?
Why did I not come as a rain,
So that I would exist always
As a bead of the cloud's breast,
To be flung to the earth
As dew or as cold snow?
I would not be doomed by my lord
So damned and so accursed!
I would be whirled back away to the sky,
Carried along as a child.
I would not need, like now
Constantly to be careful.
I would walk as the sun's worshiper
Disappointer of death;
Above the sky, below the land
I would have as my share.
I would be happy in the mountains and valleys
When I would see them turn green,
Watered with my sweat,
Flowers inside and outside,
I would open my breast
By day to the sun, at night to the moon.
I would make the dying environment
Feel the sense of life.
Transformed into snow, in my heart
The fiery desire would remain
That again my death
Would turn into life
And embrace renewed nature
By the neck.

არწივი

არწივი ვნახე დაჭრილი,
ყვავ-ყორნებს ომებოდა,
ეწადა ზეჩავს აღგომა,
მაგრამ ვეღარა დგებოდა,
ცალს მხარს მიწაზე მიითრევს,
გულისპირს სისხლი სცხებოდა.
ვაჰ, დედას თქვენსა, ყოვებო,
ცუდ დროს ჩაგიგდავთ ხელადა,
თორო ვნახავდი თქვენს ბუმბულს
გაშლილს, გაფანტულს ველადა.

Eagle by Vazha-Pshavela

Translated by Lela Jgerenaia

I saw an injured eagle,
fighting with ravens,
pitiful it was seeking to rise,
but could not stand up,
dragging one shoulder on the ground,
With blood greased on the bib.
Oh! For your mothers, ravens,
you caught me in hard time,
otherwise I would see your feathers
scattered and tossed about in the field.

გული
ნიკო ლორთქიფანიძე

მოკვდა.

დის ნაზ ხელს არ გაუსწორებია სასთუმალი; იდუმალის მწუხარებით არ შემოუხედავს ავადმყოფის ოთახში სატრფოს თვალები; ნაცნობებს არ მოუკითხავთ; უკანასკნელ წამს შენდობა არ მიუღია იმ მშვიდ, წყნარ ადამიანისაგან, რომლის ძალა აღარ სწამდა, მაგრამ დამამშვიდებელი სიტყვების მისგან გაგონება მაინც უნდოდა; დედას არ დაუყრია ცხარე ცრემლები.

მოკვდა უცხოეთში.

- ათასი სნეულებით იყო ავად, არავითარმა წამალმა არ იმოქმედა, - იმართლებდა თავს
ამხანაგთა წინაშე ექიმი.

ცხედარი გაჭრეს. პროფესორმა ხელები ჩამოუშვა და გაკვირვებულმა წამოიძახა:

- შეხედეთ, ბატონებო, ეს რა ამბავია?! ერთმანეთს შესცქეროდნენ.

- ბატონებო, გული, გული, სადღაა?

გულის მაგიერ ფეფრფლიდა დარჩენილიყო. დეპეშით გაგებული უბედურებისაგან თავზარდაცემული დედა შევიდა საყვარელ შვილის ობლად დატოვებულ ოთახში ქვითინებდა: ასე გამომიმეტე ქვრივი ოხერი? სადაა შენი კარგი გული, ამდენის ვაით და ვუით რომ ჩაგიდგი საგულეში?

კედლიდან პატარა რუქამ გასცა პასუხი:

- მე დავაჭკნე!
- მე დავწვი! - გახმაურდა სურათი მაგიდაზე.

სიტყვები არავის გაუგონია.

Heart
By Niko Lortkiphanidze
Translated by Lela Jgerenaia

Died.

The sister's tender hand did not make the bed; the sick one's lover did not drop in with mysterious grief. Friends did not give kind regards to him. At the last moment he did not receive forgiveness from that calm, quiet human being, whose power he did not believe in any longer; but still wanted to hear soothing words from; his mother did not drop bitter tears.

He died in a foreign country.

-he was sick with a thousand diseases; no medicine helped. – the doctor was excusing himself to his friends.

They cut the corpse.

The professor dropped his arms and screamed with astonishment:

-look! Gentlemen. What's going on here?!

They were staring at each other.

-Gentlemen, the heart. Where's the heart?

Instead of the heart only ashes remained. Learning about this from a telegram, horror-stricken by the misfortune the mother went into her beloved son's orphaned room. Weeping – how could he abandon me, an accursed widow? Where's your fine heart, which I put into you with all my cries of woe.

A little map gave an answer from the wall.

-I faded it.

-I burned it! – gave away the picture on the table.

Nobody heard the words.

საქართველო იყიდება

იყიდება საქართველო. მინდორ-ველით, მთა-გორით, ტყით, ვენახით, სათესით; წარსულის ისტორი-ით, მომავალი სვე-ბედით; მშვენიერის ენით; ნაქარგი ფარჩა-ხავერდით; ვაჟკაცურის ხასიათით, სტუმართ-მოყვარეობით; დიდებულის სანახაობით, წმინდა ჰაე-რით; ნაამაგევი სახლით და კარით; ჩუქურთმიანი მონას-ტრებით და ეკლესიაბით; მჩქეფარე ნაკადულებით; ლურჯის ზღვით; მოწმენდილ-მოკაშკაშებულ ცით; ერით, ბერით; თვალწარმტაც ბანოვანთა გუნდებით; გონებაგახსნილ ვაჟებით; მალხაზი ბავშვებით; ვერცხლისფერ თმით შემოსილ პატივსადებ მოხუცებით. იყიდება საქართველო დედით და მამით, შვილით და ძირით, ძმით, დით, ცოლით და ნათესავ-მოყვრებით.

ჰყიდის ყველა: თავადი, მღვდელი, ვაჭარი, ავა-ზაკი, დიდი და პატარა, ჭკვიანი და სულელი, ლოთი და პირაკრული. იყიდება ყველგან: ქუჩაში და სახლში, თეა-ტრში და სასამართლოში, სასწავლებელში, სატუსაღოში, ეტლში, მატარებელში, დილით და ღამით, სიცხეში და სიცივეში, დარში და ავდარში.

იყიდება ერთიანად: შავი ზღვიდან კასპიის ზღვამ-დე და ოსეთიდან სპარსეთამდე. იყიდება ნაწილ-ნაწილ: კახეთი და იმერეთი, ქართლი, სვანეთი და სამეგრელო, გურია და ლეჩხუმი, რაჭა და ჯავახეთი. იყიდება პატარ-პატარ ნაჭრებათ, ვისაც რამდენი სურს და როგორც უნდა: ნისიათ, უფასოდ, ნაღდად, დროებით და სამუდამოთ; ბანკის დახმარებით და ჩვენის საშუალებით. იყიდეთ ბა-რემ მთლად, გაწეწეთ და გაგლიჯეთ, რასაც საქართველო ერქვა და რაც დღეს ოხრად დარჩენილი აძეგებს ყორნებს და გულს უკლავს უძლურ ჭირისუფალს!

Georgia is being sold
by Niko Lortkipanidze
Translated by Lela Jgerenaia

Georgia is being sold with its fields and steppes, mountains and hills, forests, vineyards, ploughed fields; past history, destiny, wonderful language; with silk velvet embroidery, manly character, hospitality, magnificent scenery; pure air, laboriously prepared households, fretted monasteries and churches. Seething streams, blue sea, clear-shiny sky, nation, monks, groups of charming ladies, bright lads, lively children, silver-haired honored elders;

Georgia is being sold with mother and father, child and elder, brother, sister, wife and friends and relatives. It's being sold by everybody: nobility, priest, merchant, robber, young and old, smart and dumb, drunkard and teetotaler.

It's being sold everywhere: in the street and at home, at the cinema and at the law-court, at schools, in the prison, in a phaeton, on a train, in the morning and in the evening, in the cold and in the heat, in the fine weather and in bad weather. It is being sold entirely: from the black sea to the Caspian Sea, and from Ossetia to Persia. It's being sold piece-by-piece: Kakheti and Imereti, Kartli, Svaneti and Samegrelo, Guria and Lechkhumi, Racha and Javakheti; It's being sold in small parts. Who wants how many and how: based on a promise, for free, for cash, temporarily and permanently, using a bank and by our help.

Buy it complete, crumple it and tear it to pieces, what used to be called Georgia and now sates the ravens and kills the heart of the feeble mourner.

ჩივილი ხმლისა

ვაჟა-ფშაველა

- დაჰკანგებულხარ, გორდაო,
დაგობებია ქარქაში.
სადა გყავს შენი პატრონი,
დაგაწყებინოს კაშკაში?
- სადღა მყავს, ძმაო, პატრონი:
შამქორს გავწირე მკვდარია,
ორმოცგან სჭირდა ნახმლევი,
სდიოდა სისხლის ღვარია.
ომში წინ წასვლა უყვარდა,
ხელთ დაბღუჯვილი ფარია;
არას დასდევდა სიკვდილსა,
ოღომც არ შარცხვეს ჯარია,
მეფის თამარის გვირგვინი,
ქართველთ სამეფო გვარია.
ეხლა უშნოდ ვარ... დამკიდეს
ლაჩართ კედელზე უქმადა;
ვისღა სცალია ჩემთვისა,
ქვეყანა იქცა დუქნადა.
გადამაგდებენ გირაოდ...
და გზირ-ნაცვლების ხელითა
ქვეყანა მხედავს მდებარეს
„არშინის", „ჩოთქის" გვერდითა.
შვიდასი წელი გამიხდა,
არ გავპოხილვარ ღუმითა,
არ ვულესივარ ქართველსა
დაღიდინებით ჩუმითა.
მისი ხმა აღარ მსმენია:
„გასჭერ, გამიშვი წინაო,
თუ სახელს არ მაშრვნინებ,
როგორ დავბრუნდე შინაო!"

The Complaint of the Sword by Vazha-Pshavela

Translated by Lela Jgerenaia

- you've become rusty, sword
Your sheath has grown mouldy.
where do you have your owner,
So that he would make you shine?
-where do I have my owner, brother,
I doomed him in Shamqori, he is dead,
he had injuries in forty places,
Blood's stream was flowing.
he liked going forward in war,
with a buckler held in his hands;
He did not care about death,
only that the army should not be disgraced,
King Tamar's crown,
The Georgians' royal name.
now I'm disused... hung on the
coward's wall, idle;
who's got time for me,
The country's turned into a tavern.
I will be thrown down for a mortgage...
By the vice-regent's hand
the country sees me situated
next to yardstick, abacus.
It has been already seven-hundred years,
I haven't been treated with oil,
I haven't been sharpened by a Georgian
with quiet crooning.
I have not heard his voice:
"blade, let me go forward,
if you won't help me earn a name
how can I go back home!"

სიმღერა

(პასუხად)

მე რო ტირილი მეწადოს,
თქვენ ვის რა გინდათ, ნეტარა?
ერთი იცინის, სხვა ტირის:
ესეთი არი ქვეყანა.
ვისაც არ მოგწონსთ ტირილი,
ის ნუ დაგხდებით ჩემთანა:
მტირალის სტვირის პატრონი
ფეხს როგორ გავსწვდი თქვენთანა?!
მაგრამ გავიგებთ ერთხელაც,
ვინ ახლო ვსდგავართ მერთთანა.

A Song by Vazha-Pshavela

(As an answer)

Translated by Lela Jgerenaia

If I desired weeping
I would wonder, what do you want?
One laughs, another weeps:
The universe is of this kind.
Those who dislike crying,
should not sit next to me:
A master of a weeping fife
How can I compare my height to yours?!
But one day we will find out,
Who stands closer to God.

1886

ჩემო კალამო, ჩემო კარგო, რად გვინდა ტაში ?

ჩემო კალამო, ჩემო კარგო, რად გვინდა ტაში ?
რასაც ვმსახურებთ, მას ერთგულად კვლავ ვემსახუროთ,
ჩვენ წმინდა სიტყვა უშიშარად მოვფინოთ ხალხში
ზოროტ საკლავად მათ სულთხდომის სეირს ვუყუროთ.

თუ კაცმა ვერ სცნო ჩვენი გული, ხომ იცის ღმერთმა,
რომ წმინდა არის განზრახვა და სურვილი ჩვენი:
აგიყოლია სიყრმიდანვე ჩვენ ქართვლის ბედმა,
და დაე, გვჯერახონ ჩვენ - მის ქებნით დავლიოთ დღენი.

ჩემზედ ამბობენ: "ის, სიავეს ქართვლისას ამბობს
ჩვენს ცუდს არ მალავს, ეგ ხომ ცხადი სიმულვილია!"
ბრიყვნი ამბობენ, კარგი გული კი მაშინვე სცნობს,
!ამსიმულვილიშირაოდენიცსიყვარულია!

My Pen, My Dear, Why Do We Need Applause?
By Ilia Chavchavadze
Translated by Lela Jgerenaia

My pen, my dear, why do we need applause?
what we are serving, let's serve it devotedly again,
let's spread the pure word among the people fearlessly,
to slaughter the wicked, - with amusement let's watch their
souls' last breath.

If a man could not recognize our heart, doesn't god know it,
that our intention and desire are pure:
the destiny of Georgians dragooned us from adolescence,
And let them reproach us, - let us drink down our days in
searching for it.

They say of me: "He is speaking of evil of Georgians,
he does not conceal our faults, isn't this evidence of hatred!"
the rude people say, but the good hearted notice at once,
in this hatred how much of love there is!

ღამე

ილია ჭავჭავაძე

როცა ყაყანი ქვეყანისა სრულად მიწყდება
და აღარ ისმის ზოროტების ხმა მოსაწყენი,
როს, მთინარს-სოფელს კამარა ცის ზედ გარდეშლება
სამხრეთის ღამევ, მაშინ მიყვარს ყურება შენი!

Night by Ilia Chavchavadze

Translated by Lela Jgerenaia

when the hubbub of the nation dies away completely
and the boring voice of spite is no more heard,
when the dome of heaven lies over the sleeping country,-
Oh night of the south, then do I love watching you!

უსიყვარულოდ

უსიყვარულოდ
მზე არ სუფევს ცის კამარაზე,
სიო არ დაჰქრის, ტყე არ კრთება
სასიხარულოდ....
უსიყვარულოდ არ არსებობს
არც სილამაზე,
არც უკვდავება არ არსებობს
უსიყვარულოდ.
მაგრამ სულ სხვაა სიყვარული
უკანასკნელი,
როგორც ყვავილი შემოდგომის
ხშირად პირველს სჯობს,
იგი არ უხმობს ქარიშხლიან
უმიზნო ვნებებს,
არც ყმაწვილურ ჟინს, არც ველურ ხმებს
იგი არ უხმობს...
და შემოდგომის სიცივეში
ველად გაზრდილი,
ის გაზაფხულის ნაზ ყვავილებს
სულაც არა ჰგავს...
სიოს მაგივრად ქარიშხალი
ეალერსება
და ვნების ნაცვლად უხმო ალერსს
გარემოუცავს.
და ჭკნება, ჭკნება სიყვარული
უკანასკნელი,
ჭკნება მწუხარედ, ნაზად, მაგრამ
უსიხარულოდ.
და არ არსებობს ქვეყანაზე
თვით უკვდავება,
თვით უკვდავებაც არ არსებობს
უსიყვარულოდ!

Without Love by Galaktion Tabidze

Translated by Lela Jgerenaia

Without love
The sun does not reign in the firmament,
the breeze does not waft, the forest does not thrill
joyfully...
Without love there exists
no beauty,
nor does immortality exist
without love.
But the last love is quite
different,
as a flower of autumn
it's often better than the first,
It does not call up stormy
aimless passions,
neither adolescent whim, nor wild voices
It does not call up ...
And in the cold of the autumn
grown in the field,
It does not look like springtime tender flowers
at all......
Instead of breeze a storm
caresses it
and instead of passion voiceless endearment
has surrounded it.
and withers, withers love
the last,
withers sorrowfully, tenderly, but
joylessly.
And there does not exist in the universe
immortality itself,
even immortality itself does not exist
without love!

1914

რაც უფრო შორს ხარ
გალაკტიონ ტაბიძე

რაც უფრო შორს ხარ - მით უფრო ვტკბები!
მე შენში მიყვარს ოცნება ჩემი.
ხელუხლებელი - როგორც მზის სხივი,
მიუწვდომელი - როგორც ედემი.

და თუ არა ხარ ის, ვისაც ვფიქრობ, -
მე დღეს არ ვნაღვლობ, დაე, ვცდებოდე!
ავადმყოფ გულს სურს, რომ მას ოცნების
თეთრ ანგელოზად ევლინებოდე.

დაიწვას გული უცნაურ ტრფობით,
ცრემლით აივსოს ზღვა-საწყაული -
ოღონდ მჯეროდეს მე ჩემი ბოდვა
და სიყვარულის დღესასწაული.

1908

Farther You Are by Galaktion Tabidze
Translated by Lela Jgerenaia

The farther you are the more I delight in you
in you I love this dream of mine
inviolable like the ray of the sun
inaccessible like paradise…

and if you are not the one, I am thinking of
I have no regrets today, let me be wrong,
the suffering soul wants you to appear to it
as the white angel of dream…

let the heart burn with strange admiration,
let the sea be filled with bitter tears
if I merely believe in my own delirium
and the festival of the love…

1908

Ingeborg Bachmann
Römisches Nachtbild

Wenn das Schaukelbrett die sieben Hügel
nach oben entführt, gleitet es auch,
von uns beschwert und umschlungen,
ins finstere Wasser,

taucht in den Flußschlamm, bis in unsrem Schoß
die Fische sich sammeln.
Ist die Reihe an uns,
stoßen wir ab.

Es sinken die Hügel,
wir steigen und teilen
jeden Fisch mit der Nacht.

Keiner springt ab.
So gewiß ist's, daß nur die Liebe
und einer den andern erhöht.

Roman Night-Portrait by Ingeborg Bachmann

Translated by Megan Wilson

When the Swing kidnaps the seven Hills
upward, it also glides,
heavy and embraced by us,
into the dark Water,

dives into the River-muck, until in our Lap
the Fish collect themselves.
It is our Turn;
we recoil.

The Hills sink,
we climb and share
each Fish with the Night.

No one jumps.
For it's sure, that only Love
and one person raises another.

Találkozás egy fiatalemberrel
Karinthy Frigyes

Jókedvű voltam, sok mindent elfelejtettem, körülményesen meggyújtottam a szivarom, és nekivágtunk az Andrássy útnak. Én szép és drága feleségem mosolygott rám a fátyol alól, én szép kedvesem, aki, íme, szeretett, és megengedte, hogy szeressem. A fiatalemberrel a Duna-parton találkoztam, hat óra felé. Elment mellettünk, már alkonyodott akkor, nem vettem észre. Már húsz lépésnyire lehetett, mikor hátulról megpillantottam. Egyszerre elhallgattam, és zavart nyugtalanság fogott el. A karcsú derék egy rakodóhajó hátteréből vált ki élesen, de mégis, azt hiszem, a lépéseiről ismertem rá. Kicsit kopottak a ruhák. A kezében széles füzetet vitt. Tizennyolc vagy csak tizenhét éves talán... még haboztam, nem mertem elhinni... el akartam fordulni, de egyszerre éles nyilallás vonaglott át a szívemen, és utána oly heves dobogás fogta el, hogy meg kellett álljak. Egy mozdulatát láttam meg, amint a kezét felemelte, és maga elé tartotta, ó jaj, rettenetes, ez volt a kéz, még a vágást is megismertem rajta, amit a tornateremben... A feleségem csodálkozva nézett rám, és én hebegve mondtam:

- Kérlek... várj rám... beszélnem kell ezzel a fiatalemberrel...

És otthagytam őt és előresiettem. Nemsokára aztán meglassítottam a lépteimet. Már alkonyodott.

A fiatalember nem fordult meg. Tudta, hogy mögötte vagyok. Nyugodtan ment tovább, egy hajókötélkőnél nyugodtan megállt, és a csendes Duna felé fordult s nézett át, messze a hegyek felé. Borzasztó zavarban voltam, a torkom köszörültem. Melléje álltam, hogy észrevétessem magam. Lopva a száját néztem, mely fiatalabb és keskenyebb volt még, mint az enyém. A szeme nagyobb és világosabb. Ó, ő volt az. És a füzet a kezében, a régi füzet... amit a szekrényem fenekére tettem és elfelejtettem... Nehéz, szorongó izgalom volt ez.

- Hát... nem látsz?... - mondtam végre halkan.

- De igen - mondta, de nem fordult felém.

147

Encounter with a Young Man
Karinthy Frigyes
Translated by Fanni Török

I was in a good mood, I forgot about everything, I painstakingly lit my cigar and we headed toward Andrassy[2]. My beautiful and dear wife smiled at me from under her veil, my beautiful sweetheart, who, loved me and let me love her. I encountered the young man on the bank of the Danube around six o'clock. He walked past us, it was already dusk by then, and I didn't notice him. He was about twenty paces behind us when I recognized him from behind. Suddenly, I became quiet and a vague sense of unease grabbed a hold of me. The slim waist was sharply silhouetted against a carrier ship, but still, I think I recognized him by his gait. Clothes a bit worn. He carried a large notebook in his hand. Perhaps eighteen or maybe just seventeen years old…I hesitated, I didn't dare to believe it…I wanted to turn away, but suddenly a sharp jolt coursed through my heart only to be followed by such intense palpitations that I had to stop walking. I saw him move as he lifted his hand in front of him…Oh, why it was *the* hand, I even recognized the cut, the one from gym class…

My wife looked at me curiously as I stuttered, "Please…wait for me…I need to speak with that young man…

And I left her there and hurried ahead. Soon, I began to slow my steps. It was almost dusk. The young man did not turn around. He knew I was behind him. He calmly went ahead and stopped by a mooring, turned toward the calm Danube and looked into the distance toward the mountains. I was horribly embarrassed and clearing my throat. I stood next to him to make my presence more noticeable. I was watching his mouth out of the corner of my eye, a mouth that looked much thinner and younger than mine. His eyes were larger and clearer. Yes, it was him. And in his hand, the old notebook…which I placed in the bottom of my drawer and have long forgotten…This was certainly a heavy, anxious excitement.

"Can't you see me?" I finally asked quietly.

"Yes," he replied, but did not turn toward me.

---

[2] Andrassy Avenue is a famous boulevard in Budapest.

Zavartan hallgattam. Aztán elszégyelltem magam. Nevetséges. Egy tizennyolc eves fiatalember! A találkozás különös, de fel kell találjam magam. Elfogulatlan leszek. Örüljön, hogy alkalma volt meglátni engem.

- Azonnal megismertelek - mondtam hangosan -, amint elmentél mellettem.

- Tudom - mondta.

- Hát mért nem jöttél oda? Nem vagy kíváncsi rám?

Nem felelt. Ideges lettem.

- Jó, tudom, milyen tartózkodó és gőgös vagy. De látod, ennek semmi értelme... Hidd el, rájöttem, hogy semmi értelme... Majd elmagyarázom neked... Magad is belátod majd, hogy nem maradhattam tartózkodó és gőgös... De hát miért nem nézel rám... Nézd, bajuszom van... Huszonhat éves vagyok... De furcsa vagy. Haragszol rám? Nem felelt. A szája keserűen összehúzódott.

- Eh!... - mondtam. - Ez a nagyszerű hallgatás! Jó, jó, emlékszem már... Hát aztán? Örökké

nem csinálhatja azt az ember. Né, még talán szemrehányásokat teszel. Ugyan kérlek, a nagy

hallgatásod nem olyan nagy dolog... Nem látom, hogy sokat használt neked... A ruhád nagyon

74

szánalmas, édes fiam. És sovány vagy. Már engedj meg, nem tudnék ilyen ruhát felvenni...

Na, mi az! Sírj egy kicsit, kapsz egy krajcárt!

Most nézett rám először. Keményen rám nézett, a szemembe. Aztán megint elfordult.

- Sokat beszélsz - mondta szárazan.

Megsértődtem.

- Ó! Ugyan! Nagyon tökéletesnek képzeled magad. Igenis, beszélek, mert tanítani akarlak...

érted? Végre, idősebb vagyok nálad... és én azóta sokat láttam... és sokat tapasztaltam... te

gyerek vagy... mit tudod te...

Egyszerre elcsuklott a hangom, lehorgasztottam a fejem, és egészen halkan és zavartan mosolyogtam,

149

I waited in confusion. Then I felt ashamed. Laughable. An eighteen year old! The encounter is peculiar, but I have to compose myself. I will be objective. He ought to be happy to have the opportunity to see me.

"I recognized you immediately," I said loudly. "As soon as you walked past me."

"I know," he said.

"Well why didn't you approach me? Aren't you curious about me?"

He didn't reply and I became agitated.

"All right, I know how introverted and arrogant you are. But you see there is no point in acting this way. Believe me, I realized that there is no point...I'll tell you...You'll see that I couldn't stay introverted and arrogant...But why won't you look at me...Look, I have a mustache...I'm twenty-six years old...you are so strange. Are you mad at me?"

He didn't reply. His mouth became bitter and drawn.

"Oh!" I said. "These meaningful silences! Fine, fine, I remember now...So what? One can't do the same thing forever. And you are reproaching me. Oh please, your great silences are not as great as you think...I don't see the good they have done you...Your clothes are in a sorry state, son. And you're thin. Excuse me, but I couldn't wear those clothes anymore...Oh, what's wrong! Cry a bit and you'll get a penny!"

He now looked at me for the first time. He looked me coldly in the eyes and then turned away.

"You talk a lot," he remarked wryly. I was offended.

"Oh, please! You think you are perfect. Yes I talk, because I want to teach you...understood? I am finally older than you...and I have seen a lot since then...and I have experienced a lot...you are a child...what do you know..." Suddenly, my voice faltered, I hung my head and I quietly lifted my arms

és halkan és zavartan felemeltem a kezem, és zavartan mosolyogva suttogtam:

- ...Hát mit tegyek?... hát azt nem lehetett, ahogy te gondoltad. Hidd el, kérlek, nem lehetett... én próbáltam... de igazán nem lehetett... Most felém fordult. Elgörbült szájjal, gyűlölettel nézett rám.

- Hol a repülőgép? - kérdezte rekedten.

Zavartan dadogtam:

- Hát... mit tegyek... feltalálták... Farman... a Wright-testvérek... nem voltam ott... De hidd el,

ők is elég jól csinálták... egész jó, aránylag... lehet vele repülni...

- Látom - mondta gúnyosan. Aztán megint rám nézett. - Hol az Északi-sark?

Lesütöttem a szemem:

- Valami Peary elérte... Kérlek, hát nem volt időm... te tévedtél... nem lehet mindent... én

akkor az egyetemre jártam...

- Úgy - mondta.

Aztán:

- Hol a büszke és szabad Magyarország?

- Kérlek alássan... igazán furcsa vagy... dolgozunk rajta... én is... de az nem megy olyan

hamar... az embernek élni is kell.

Hadarni kezdtem:

- De látod... azért én igyekeztem... hogy legyen valami abból... amit neked, megígértem... írtam ám. Elég jó dolgokat írtam... Nézd meg csak kérlek a kirakatokat... a nevem ismerik... jónevű vagyok... ahogy te akartad... és az emberek eléggé tisztelnek... És látod, könyveket is írtam... ahogy te elgondoltad... nézd csak... itt van egy... elég jó... Idegesen kapkodtam ki a zsebemből egyik könyvemet, amiben humoros rajzok és novella vannak, és mutattam neki.

- Nézd csak... elég jó...

Egyetlen pillantást vetett csak a könyvre, nem nyúlt utána.

- Igen, láttam már - mondta kurtán. - Elég jó. Kinyújtotta a karját az alkonyodó láthatár, az elgörbülő hegyek felé.

151

and with a confused smile whispered: "What am I to do?...it couldn't be the way you imagined it. Please believe me, it couldn't be...I just tried...but it really couldn't be..."

Now he turned to me. He frowned as he looked at me with hate. "Where is the airplane?" he asked hoarsely.

"Well...what am I to do...they invented it...some Farman[3]...the Wright brothers[4]...I wasn't there...But believe me, they did a good enough job...it's quite good, ...you can fly with it..."

"I see," he said mockingly. Then he looked at me again. "Where is the North Pole?"

I cast my eyes down.

"Some Peary[5] reached it...Please, there was no time...you were mistaken...one can't do everything...I was going to college then."

"Indeed," he said.

"Where is the proud and free Hungary?"

"I beg you please...you are quite strange...we're working on it...I am too...but it can't happen so soon...a person has to live."

I began to jabber:

"But you see...I did try...to accomplish some things I had promised you...I wrote...I wrote well enough...Please, look at that display window...they know my name...I have a good name...just as you wanted...and people quite respect me...And see, I wrote books, just like you imagined...Look here is one...it's quite good..."

I nervously pulled one of my books, one with humorous illustrations and short stories, out of my pocket and showed it to him.

"Look...it's quite good..."

He took one glance at the book but did not reach for it.

"Yes, I have already seen it," he said. "It's quite good."

He swept his arm across the landscape, pointing toward the dusky horizon and the curving mountains.

---

[3] Richard, Henri and Maurice Farman founded Farman Aviation Works in France and designed and constructed airplanes until the 1930s.

[4] Orville and Wilbur Wright were the first to invent the airplane.

[5] Robert Peary was an American explorer and the first to reach the geographic North Pole.

75

- Hol a nagy szimfónia, a rettenetes színjáték a szürke láthatárról és a gőgös istenekről, akik ott lüktetnek és vonaglanak a láthatár mögött?

Elpirultam.

- Hát, kérlek... azt nem lehetett... Azt nem lehet három felvonásban megcsinálni... Te tévedtél... A szürke láthatárt nem tudja eljátszani egy színész... aztán rájöttem, hogy ez nem is a megfelelő műfaj... és nem is tudnék elkészülni vele... Hanem írtam erről egy csinos szonettet... egy előkelő revü hozta... és tetszett... és azóta jobban fizetnek... Nem felelt. Komor hallgatásba merült, tekintete eltűnt a távolban. Akartam még mondani valamit, megmagyarázni, hogy milyen fiatal ő... de homályosan emlékeztem rá, hogy ilyenkor, mikor így néz, nem lehet őt zavarni. Egyszerre eszembe jutott a feleségem, és nyugtalankodni kezdtem.

- Kérlek... - mondtam - jöjj velem, bemutatlak a feleségemnek. Ó, ennek örülni fogsz. Nagyon szép asszony... értékes, nagyszerű nő... látod... és én meghódítottam... szeret engem... látod... vagyok valaki... ahogy te akartad...

Most rám nézett, és a szemében végtelen gúny volt.

- Meghódítottad - mondta. - Ugyan! Ó, milyen büszke vagy rá! Te mentél hozzá és meghódítottad!...

A várkastély leszállt a hegyről, és ostrommal bevette a völgyet!... A tölgy meghódította a folyondárt, és szerelmesen körülcsavarta... Miért nem jön ide a feleséged?

Összehúztam a szemem.

- Ostoba vagy - mondtam. - Gyerek vagy. Ezek fantazmagóriák. Nincs igazad. Nekem van igazam. Én felnőtt vagyok, és megismertem az életet. Mit tudsz te az életről! Téged mindenki kinevetne!

Egészen mellém állt, a szemembe nézett. Most láttam meg sűrű és barna haját.

- Nem akartam megismerni az életet... azt akartam, hogy az élet ismerjen meg engem... Igaz, engem mindenki kinevetne, és te nem akartad, hogy miattam téged kinevessenek...

153

"Where is the great symphony, the tragic drama about the grey horizon and arrogant gods, who throb and thrash beyond the horizon?"

I blushed.

"Please...it couldn't be...You can't do that in three acts...You were mistaken...An actor can't play 'the grey horizon'...and then I realized that it isn't even the ideal genre...and I wouldn't even be able to finish it...But I wrote a sonnet about it...with an elegant revue of it...and they liked it...and they pay me better since..."

He didn't reply. He sunk into a deep silence as he gazed into the distance. I wanted to say something more, to explain how young he is...but I vaguely remembered that when he looks like this, he cannot be disturbed. Suddenly, I remembered my wife and began to fidget.

"Please...," I said. "Come with me, I'll introduce you to my wife. Oh, you will like this. She's a beautiful woman...a precious, wonderful woman...you'll see...I'm somebody....just as you wanted..."

He now looked at me mockingly.

"You think you conquered her," he said. "Please! You are so proud of her! You were the one who went to her, and you think you conquered her!...Just as a fort can lift itself of the hill and with a charge cover the valley!...Just as the oak conquered the ivy as it lovingly wound it around itself...Why won't your wife come here?"

I narrowed my eyes.

"You are a fool," I said. "You are a child. These are fantasies. You're not right. I am right. I am the grown-up and I have gotten to know life. What do you know about life! Everyone would laugh at you!"

He stood quite close to me and looked into my eyes. I just now noticed his thick brown hair.

"I didn't want to get to know life...what I wanted was for life to get to know me...Yes, everyone would laugh at me and you didn't want people to laugh at you because of me...

De te tudod, nézz a szemembe, merj a szemembe nézni!... te tudod, hogy te vagy a nevetséges és kicsi... és hogy nekem van igazam... és hogy nem nevetséges, amit én mondok... te tudod, hogy nekem van igazam... te szegény... te kicsi... te senki... Merj a szemembe nézni...

El kellett fordulnom; a helyzet ostoba és kínos volt. Ő lassan távolodott el tőlem, aztán nem nézett többé rám, lassan, gondolkodva indult meg... Percek múlva, halkan tudtam csak megszólalni:

- Hová mész? Maradj... - suttogtam. De nem fordult már vissza. Csak a szavát hallottam még,

távolról:

- Emlékezz rá, hogy egyszer még, utoljára, találkoztál velem... És ha van még benned valami belőlem, mártsd be tolladat a lenyugvó nap tüzébe, s írd meg nekik... írd meg ezt a találkozást... és írd meg nekik, hogy hagytalak el, és hogy tűntem el, beleolvadva az alkonyodó égbe, ifjan, szépen és végtelenül szabadon, hogy ne lássalak többé... Ezeket nagyon messziről hallottam már, és a karcsú alak vékonyodott, elfolyt, felemelkedett. Még néztem, azt hittem, hogy látom, de aztán rájöttem, hogy a vörös égen egy vékony felhő lebeg csak.

A feleségem türelmetlen lett.

- Ki volt ez a fiatalember? - kérdezte.

76

- Egy régi ismerősöm - mondtam neki zavartan. - Kedves fiú...

- Igen - mondta a feleségem kicsit élesen. - Csak rossz modora van. Miért nem mutatkozik be?

Pedig feltűnően hasonlít hozzád.

Aztán idejöttünk a kávéházba. Nehéz kedvemről lassan oszolt el a görcs. A téma szép - mondtam magamban, felvidulva. - Versnek kicsit hosszú volna. De egy novella lehet belőle csinálni. Röviden, szatirikusan. Ma úgyis kedd van, szállítanom illik valamit.

Papírt kértem, és rövid habozás után leírtam a címet: „Találkozás egy fiatalemberrel...”

És csak tompán fájt már a seb.

155

But you know... look into my eyes, dare to look into my eyes!...but you know that you are the one that is laughable and small...and that I am right...and that what I say is not laughable...you know I am right...you wretch...you small...you nobody...I dare you to look me in the eyes...

I had to turn away; the situation was silly and awkward. He slowly distanced himself from me, no longer staring at me and slowly and deliberately began to walk away....

Minutes later, I could only whisper:

"Where are you going? Stay..." But he didn't turn around. I only heard his voice from the distance.

"Remember, that an additional and final time, you met with me...And if there is still something from me in you, dip your pen into the fire of the setting sun, and write it for them...write about this encounter...and tell them how I left you and how I disappeared, melting into the dusky sky, young, beautiful and forever free, never to see you again..."

I heard these words from far away and the slim figure thinned, wasted and rose. I watched, thinking I saw him, but then realized the shadow was only a hovering strip of red cloud.

My wife became impatient.

"Who was this young man?" she asked.

"An old acquaintance," I replied, perplexed. "Nice kid..."

"Yes," my wife said a bit sharply. "But with bad manners. Why didn't he introduce himself? And he looked remarkably like you."

Then, we came here to the cafe. The anxious knot inside me melted slowly away from my heavy mood.

"The topic is nice," I said to myself, happily. "A bit too long for a poem. But I could write a short story. Brief and satirical. Today is Tuesday, anyway, I should deliver them something."

I asked for paper and after brief hesitation wrote down the title; "Encounter with a Young Man..."

And now the pain in my wound began to dull.

Hány óra van fiam?!...
Hunyadi Sándor

U. úr már felnőtt ember, előkelő rangja van az egyik minisztérium státusában. De tizenöt évvel ezelőtt még kisdiák volt, az hiszem, Debrecenben járt iskolába. Akkor történt, hogy kapott ajándekba egy tula-ezüstből készült zsebórát az édesapjától, aki református pap volt a városban vagy talán csak a megyeben.

Lánca nem volt az órának, cask rojtja, szép piros selyemből. A fiú nagyon büszke volt tulajdonára, minden pillanatban megnézte, hogy mennyi az idő? Így érkezett el a nyár, amikor is az óra által okozott boldogsághoz új gyönyörűség társult. A tiszteletes úr fölhozta a fiát a pesti vásárra. Hadd lásson egy kis világot a gyerek, nem járt még túl a Hajdú megye határain.

Kimentek a kiállításra, azt hiszem, ott volt akkor is, ahol mostan van. Sodródtak a tömegben, néha megálltak, nézelődtek. Az apa élénken magyarázgatott gyermekének. Pedig ő sem volt pesti ember, sőt nagyon is lerítt bajszos, kedves arcáról, egész magatartásáról az ártatlan, barátságos és becsületes vidék.

Séta közben véletlenül ráesett a fia tula-órájának piros bojtjára a tisztelestes úr pillantása. Gondolt egy merészet, és amíg a gyerek a pavilonok kirakatait bámulta, óvatosan kihúzta piros bojtjánál fogva a lajbizsebből az órát, és elsüllyesztette a saját zsebében.

Várt néhány percig, aztán ravaszul megkérdezte:

—Hány óra van, Sanyi?!

A kisdiák udvariasan a mellenyéhez nyúlt, de persze nem volt sehol, sem bojt, sem óra. Ijedten végigkaparászta az összes zsebeit, megtapogatta magát, még a földet is megnézte köröskörül. Semmi eredmény. Torkát szorongatta a sírás, mert szörnyű fájdalom az ilyesmi. Majd kétsegbeesett hangon jelentette ki:

What Time is It, Son?
Hunyady Sándor
Translated by Fanni Török

Mr. X was a grown man with a distinguished post in one of the ministries. But fifteen years ago he was just a young schoolboy, I believe in Debrecen. That was when he received, as a gift, a sterling silver pocket watch from his father, who was a Protestant minister in the city or perhaps just in the county.

The watch didn't have a chain but just a ribbon of red silk. The boy was very proud of his new possession, and constantly checked the time. Then, in the summer, another treat followed that of the watch. The reverend brought his son to the fair in Budapest, to let the kid see some of the world; he'd never been past the borders of the county.

They went to the exhibitions; I believe it was where they still hold it today. They flowed with the crowds, occasionally pausing to look around. The father was animatedly lecturing his son, even though he himself wasn't from Pest and his mustachioed and kind face and entire demeanor revealed the innocence, friendliness and honesty of the country.

During their walk, the reverend happened to glance at the bright red ribbon peaking out of the boy's pocket. Boldly, while the boy was admiring the displays, he carefully pulled the watch by the red cord from his pocket and quickly buried it in his own coat pocket.

He waited for a few minutes, and then slyly asked:

"What time is it, Alex?"

The little boy politely reached into his vest pocket, but of course it wasn't there, neither the ribbon nor the watch. Alarmed, he anxiously riffled through all of his pockets and even looked on the ground about himself in vain. His throat began to tighten in the grasp of oncoming tears due to the horrible pain. Then he frantically declared:

—Ellopták, apa, az órámat!

A tiszteletes úr hümmögött, rosszallóan csóválta a fejét. És szép, cifra, bölcsességtől súlyos prédikációt tartott a gyereknek. Elmagyarázta, hogy mindenkinek úgy kell vigyázni a tárgyaira, mint a jó pásztornak a báránykaira. Különösképpen az olyan nagyvárosban kell vigyázni, mint Budapest, mert a világ hivalkodó nagyvárosai mind teli vannak bűnnel. Veszélyes az efféle csődületben olyan csábitó dolgokat lógatni figyelmetlenül, mint a piros bojt.

A gyerek egyre bánatosabban hallgatta az apja zengzetes korholását, végül két nagy, sós könnycsepp jelent meg a szeme sarkában.

Ekkor a tiszteletes úr úgy vélte, hogy elég lesz a leckéből, vigasztaló barackot nyomott a fia fejebúbjára, és barátságos zenére fordítva a hangjat, így szólott:

—Ne sírj, Sanyi! Én vettem el az órádat! Csak meg akartalak tanítani rá, hogy az embernek vigyázni kell! Nagyon vigyázni!

Azzal belenyúlt a zsebébe, hogy visszaadja az órát, de annak már hűlt helye volt. Egész komolyan ellopta rögtön egy jószemű tolvaj, aki láthatta a jelenetet, talán még hallgatott is néhány mondatot abból a nevelésügyi előadásból, amelyet a tiszteletes úr tartott okulás végett a gyermekének.

"Someone has stolen my watch, father!"

The reverend hummed and shook his head. And he held a beautiful wisdom-filled lecture for the child. He explained that everyone must watch their things, as the good shepherd watches his little lambs. One must be especially careful in a big city, such as Budapest, because the world's showy big cities are full of crime and sin. It is dangerous, in such a place, to carelessly display such tempting trinkets as a bright red ribbon.

The child was listening to his father's sonorous scolding, increasingly filled with remorse, until finally two salty teardrops appeared in the corner of his eye.

At this time the reverend deemed the lesson adequate, consolingly rubbed his son's head and with a suddenly friendly tone in his voice said:

"Don't cry, Alex! I took your watch! I just wanted to teach you that one must be careful! Very careful!"

With this, he reached into his pocket, to give back the watch, only to find it empty. This time it was "really" stolen by a hawk-eyed pick-pocket, who must have seen the whole scene, perhaps even listened to a few sentences of the parenting lecture, which the reverend meant as a lesson for his child.

Karácsony előtt
Gádor Béla

Már négy héttel karácsony előtt megkezdődik nálunk a gondolatolvasás korszaka. Ez annyit jelent, hogy egymás gondolatai között olvasva próbáljuk kitalálni, leginkább mit óhajtana karácsonyra a másik. Ugyanis az ősi szabályok szerint az ajándéknak meglepetésnek kell lennie, különben megette a fene az egészet. Tehát élesen figyeljük egymást, minden szót, minden mozdulatot mérlegre teszünk, ennek következtében csakhamar olyan süket, rejtjeles társalgás kap lábra, amelynek már csak mi tudjuk az értelmét.

Tegyük fel, hogy ebédnél ülünk, és behozzák a levest. Én az mondom:

—Milyen jó illata van ennek a levesnek, jobb ez, mint a legjobb francia parfüm...

Közben élesen figyelem a feleségem, hogy reagál a "parfüm" szóra. De ő megszólal, és azt mondja:

—Érdekes, nekem nem ízlik a leves...

Ez annyit jelent, hogy nem akar parfümöt, és mehetünk tovább. Aztán ő ügyeskedik. Sápadt vagy es szörös—azt mondja nekem. Talán nem jó a borotvakészüléked? Mire én azzal felelek:

—A szputnyik még mindig kering. Ijesztő a technika fejlődése.

Ez annyit jelent, hogy nem akarok villanyborotvát.

Az idén ezek a rejtjeles beszélgetések annyira összekuszultak, olyan komplikáltakká váltak, hogy már nem ismertük ki magunkat. Egy példa. Azt mondja a feleségem egy hete:

—Hideg telet jósolnak...

Before Christmas
Gádor Béla
Translated by Fanni Török

Four weeks before Christmas, the season of mind-reading begins at our house. This simply means that we try to read each other's thoughts in order to determine what the other person most desires for Christmas. In accordance with the ancient customs, the gift should be a surprise or there's no point to the whole thing. Therefore, we intently observe each other, every word and every move is weighed in and analyzed, resulting in a riddled conversation that only we know the meaning of.

Say for example, that we are sitting at lunch, and the soup is brought in. And I say; "My, this soup smells wonderful, more fragrant than the finest French perfume..."
Meanwhile, I am watching my wife to see how she reacts to the word "perfume". But she just says; "That's funny, I don't think it tastes very good..."

This simply means that she doesn't want perfume and we can move on. Then she tries her hand at the maneuver. "You're pale and have too much stubble," she tells me. "Perhaps your razor isn't working?"
To which I reply; "The Sputnik is still orbiting. These new developments in technology are astounding."
Which just means, that I don't want an electric razor.
This year, the puzzling conversations have become so mixed up, so complicated, that even we were getting caught in its webs. An example. A week ago my wife tells me;
"They're forecasting a cold winter..."

Világos, hogy jégeralsót vagy meleg zoknit akar venni. Én viszont nem akarok sem ezt, sem azt, hanem inkább valami olyan ajándékot szeretek, ami látszik, amivel lehet hencegni. Na de most, ha én egyszerűen csak azt mondom, hogy "ezek az időjósok mindig tévednek", ravaszságunk mostani állása szerint ez mindent jelenthet, tehát azt is, hogy meleg holmikat akarok kapni, holott nem akarok meleg holmikat kapni. Éppen ezért ravasz tervet eszeltem ki: másnap elmentem a boltba, és vettem magamnak egy jégeralsót és három pár meleg zoknit, hogy kikapcsoljam a lehetőséget. De mit látok a következő nap? Hogy a feleségem is rájött a trükkre, és vett maganak egy húsdarálót meg egy papucsot. Erre én vettem magamnak egy pár kalucsnit és egy bicskát. Mire ő másnap megjelent egy hajszárító géppel és egy kiló mazsolával. Én vettem korcsolyát és termoszt, ő vett manikűrkészletet és egy krumplinyomót. Én vettem fűnyíró gépet és lúdtalpbetétet, ő vett salátástálat es muffot. E pillanatban az a helyzet, hogy megvettünk magunknak egy csomó dolgot, amit nem akarunk kapni karácsonyra, de nincs egy vasunk sem. S még hozzá sajnos, ma este a feleségem azt mondta, hogy régebben a férfiak ízlésesebben öltöztek. Holnap kérek kölcsön pénzt, és veszek magamnak cilindert és lakkcipőt, mert nem szeretném, ha a feleségem karácsonyra cilindert és lakkcipőt venne nekem.

It is clear, that she wants to buy me thermal underwear or warm socks. I, however, do not want either this or that and would rather get a present I can show off. But if I now simply say that "these meteorologists are always mistaken," in our current situation this can mean anything, even that I do want warm underclothes, whereas I don't want to get warm underclothes. This is exactly why I came up with my clever plan; the next day I went to the store and bought myself a pair of thermal underwear and three pairs of warm socks, thus ruling out the possibility. But what do I see the next day? That my wife has caught on to the trick and bought herself a meat grinder and a pair of slippers. In response, I bought myself a pair of galoshes and a pocketknife. Thereupon, she came home the next day with a blow-dryer and two pounds of raisins. I bought ice-skates and a thermos, she bought a manicure-set and a potato masher. I bought a lawn-mower and arch-support insoles, she bought a salad-bowl and a muff[6]. At this moment, our situation is that we've bought ourselves a bunch of stuff that we don't want for Christmas, and don't have two pennies to rub together. And unfortunately, my wife just said that back in the day men used to dress more elegantly. So, tomorrow, I will borrow some money and buy myself a top-hat and a pair of oxford shoes, because I don't want my wife to buy me a top-hat and oxfords for Christmas.

---

[6] muff: a covering of fur or cloth, usually cylindrical, into which the hands are thrust from opposite ends to keep them warm. (*The New International Webster's Student Dictionary*)

Supplica a mia madre
Pier Paolo-Pasolini

E' difficile dire con parole di figlio
ciò a cui nel cuore ben poco assomiglio.

Tu sei la sola al mondo che sa, del mio cuore,
ciò che è stato sempre, prima d'ogni altro amore.

Per questo devo dirti ciò ch'è orrendo conoscere:
è dentro la tua grazia che nasce la mia angoscia.

Sei insostituibile. Per questo è dannata
alla solitudine la vita che mi hai data.

E non voglio esser solo. Ho un'infinita fame
d'amore, dell'amore di corpi senza anima.

Perché l'anima è in te, sei tu, ma tu
sei mia madre e il tuo amore è la mia schiavitù:

ho passato l'infanzia schiavo di questo senso
alto, irrimediabile, di un impegno immenso.

Era l'unico modo per sentire la vita,
l'unica tinta, l'unica forma: ora è finita.

Sopravviviamo: ed è la confusione
di una vita rinata fuori dalla ragione.

Ti supplico, ah, ti supplico: non voler morire.
Sono qui, solo, con te, in un futuro aprile…

Plea to my mother by Pier Paolo-Pasolini

Translated by Ali Rucker

It's hard to say with a son's words
What I am like in my heart
You are the only one on earth who knows
What my heart has always been, before any other love.
So I must tell you something horrendous to know:
It is from your grace my suffering is born.

You're irreplaceable. And so the life
that you gave me is damned to solitude.
I don't want to be alone. I have an infinite
hunger for love, for the love of bodies without souls:

Because the soul is in you, it is you, just you
you are my mother, your love is my servitude
I spent my childhood slave to this feeling
high, irredeemable, immense obligation
It was the one way to experience life
the only form, the sole color: and now it's over.

We will survive: but it's the confusion
of a life reborn outside of reason

Oh, I beg you, I beg you: don't seek to die
I'm here, alone, with you, in a future April...

못 - 날개

우린 떨어질 것을 알면서도
더 높은 곳으로만 날았지
처음 보는 세상은 너무 아름답고 슬펐지
우린 부서질 것을 알면서도
더 높은 곳으로만 날았지
함께 보낸 날들은 너무 행복해서 슬펐지
우린 차가운 바람에 아픈 날개를 서로 숨기고
약속도 다짐도 없이 시간이 멈추기만 바랐어
우린 부서질 것을 알면서도
더 높은 곳으로만 날았지
함께 보낸 날들은 너무 행복해서 슬펐지
우린 서툰 날갯짓에 지친 어깨를 서로 기대고
깨지 않는 꿈 속에서 영원히 꿈꾸기만 바랐어
우린 떨어질 것을 알면서도
더 높은 곳으로만 날았지
처음 보는 세상은 너무 아름답고 슬펐지

Nail – Wing

Translated by Ji-Su Park

We knew we were about to fall,
but we still flew towards the higher place.
The world we saw for the first time
was so beautiful and sad.

We knew we were about to break apart,
but we still flew towards the higher place.
The days we spent together were sad
because we used to be so happy back then.

We hid our aching wings in the cold wind,
hoping without any promises
that time would stop.

We knew we were about to break apart,
but we still flew towards the higher place.
The days we spent together were sad
because we used to be so happy back then.

We leaned on each other's shoulders
that were tired from the poor flaps of the wings,
and we hoped that we would dream
forever in an eternal dream.

We knew we were about to fall,
but we still flew towards the higher place.
The world we saw for the first time
was so beautiful and sad…

이장혁 - 스무살

내가 알던 형들은 하나둘 날개를 접고
아니라던 곳으로 조금씩 스며들었지
난 아직 고갤 흔들며 형들이 찾으려했던
그 무언가를 찾아 낯선 길로 나섰어
이해할 수 없었던 세상의 수상한 질서
하지만, 난 상관없는 듯
너는 말이 없었고 나는 취해있었어
우리에겐 그런게 익숙했던 것처럼
귀찮은 숙제같은 그런 나를 보면서
더이상 어떤 말도 넌 하기 싫었겠지
내가 말한 모든 건 내 속의 알콜처럼
널 어지럽게 만들고
밖으로 밖으로 너는 나가버리고
안으로 안으로 나는 혼자 남겨져
밖으로 밖으로 널 잡고 싶었지만
안으로 안으로 나는 취해만 갔어
어둡고 축축한 그 방안 그녀는 옷을 벗었고
차가운 달빛아래 그녀는 하얗게 빛났어
나는 그녀 속으로 빠져들고 있었고
창밖이 밝아왔을때 난 모든걸 알았지
그녀가 예뻤냐고, 그녀의 이름이 뭐냐고
가끔 넌 내게 묻지만...
밖으로 밖으로 사람들이 지나고
안으로 안으로 그녀는 잠들어있어
밖으로 밖으로 달아나고 싶었지만
안으로 안으로 우린 벌거벗었어
밖으로 밖으로 눈부신 태양이 뜨고
안으로 안으로 날 비추던 그햇살
밖으로 밖으로 난 아무렇지 않은 듯
안으로 안으로 하지만 난 울고 있었어
난 울고 있었어 난 울고 있었어
난 울고 있었어 난 울고 있었어...

Lee Jang Hyuk – Twenty Years Old *(Translated by Ji-Su Park)*

All the guys I knew
folded their wings one by one, and
gradually blended into the spaces
that they used to refuse before.
Still shaking my head, I took an unfamiliar road,
searching for that something these guys had been trying to find.
The doubtful order of the world always confused me
but whatever, I don't care…
You were speechless and I was drunk;
we were used to it.
Staring at me as if I were some annoying homework,
you probably didn't want to say a word to me anymore.
Everything I said made you dizzy
like alcohol inside me…
Into the outside, outside, you went out
In the inside, inside, I was left alone
In the outside, outside, I wanted to hold you, but
in the inside, inside, I was just getting drunk.
In that dark, damp room
she took off her clothes.
Under the cold moonlight she shone brightly.
I was sinking into her and when the morning dawned
bright outside the window,
I realized everything.
At times you ask me if she was pretty,
what her name was…
In the outside, outside, people are passing by
In the inside, inside, she is asleep.
Into the outside, outside, I wanted to escape, but
in the inside, inside, we are just naked.
In the outside, outside, the blinding sun rises
In the inside, inside, that sun that used to shine upon me
In the outside, outside, I pretend as if I'm okay, but
in the outside, outside I am crying.
I was crying, I was crying, I was crying, I was crying…

패닉 – 달팽이

집에 오는 길은 때론 너무 길어 나는 더욱더 지치곤 해
문을 열자마자 잠이 들었다가 깨면 아무도 없어
좁은 욕조 속에 몸을 뉘었을때 작은 달팽이 한 마리가
내게로 다가와 작은 목소리로 속삭여줬어
언젠가 먼 훗날에 저 넓고 거칠은
세상 끝 바다로 갈거라고
아무도 못봤지만 기억 속 어딘가
들리는 파도소리 따라서
나는 영원히 갈래
모두 어딘가로 차를 달리는 길 나는 모퉁이 가게에서
담배 한 개비와 녹는 아이스크림 들고 길로 나섰어
해는 높이 떠서 나를 찌르는데 작은 달팽이 한마리가
어느새 다가와 내게 인사하고 노랠 흥얼거렸어
내 모든 걸 바쳤지만 이젠 모두 푸른 연기처럼
산산이 흩어지고
내게 남아 있는 작은 힘을 다해 마지막 꿈속에서
모두 잊게 모두 잊게 해줄 바다를 건널거야...
언젠가 먼 훗날에 저 넓고 거칠은
세상 끝 바다로 갈거라고
아무도 못봤지만 기억 속 어딘가
들리는 파도소리 따라서
나는 영원히 갈래...

Panic – Snail *(Translated by Ji-Su Park)*

The walk back home feels too long sometimes
that I get even more tired.
I fall asleep as soon as I open the door, and
there's nobody when I wake up.

When I was lying in a tiny bath tub,
a tiny snail came to me and
whispered to me in its tiny voice:

Someday in a distant future,
you will go to that large, wild ocean
at the edge of the world.

Nobody has seen it yet,
but following the sound of the waves,
I will be going there forever.

While everyone was going somewhere in a car,
I picked up a cigarette and melting ice cream
at a store in a corner and
went out to a road.

While the sun was up high poking me,
a tiny snail came to me and said hi,
and started singing:

I sacrificed everything I had,
but now everything has scattered away
like blue smoke.
With a tiny amount of strength that's left within me,
I will cross the ocean
that will make me forget everything
in my final dream…

Someday in distant future,
you will go to that large, wild ocean
at the edge of the world.

Nobody has seen it yet,
but following the sound of the waves,
I will be going there forever…

에픽하이 - 숨을 쉬어 (미쓰라의 말)

꿈이란 달콤해
겨울 지나간 봄에 피는 꽃처럼
남몰래 맘고생 끝에 미소 감도네
사회란 시선안에 어긋나며
"관둬, 얘!"
부모님의 강요에 때만 찌들어 간 소매
사회가 진정 원하는경험 그것은
책에선 볼 수 없는 비밀정원
몸이 스스로 느끼고 피부로 숨쉬고
손발이 부르터가도 아름다운 시도
내 아이만큼은 더 크게 키우고싶어
무거운 부담감을 학원으로 밀어
어떻게든 되겠지 과외로 힘 실어주면돼
근데 왜 자꾸 눈빛을 잃어
보고픈 것은 다 자꾸 막아두니까
내 젊음의 계획조차 남이 다 짜주니까
숨이차 다들 경쟁에 지쳤어
더 이상 아이들이 설 자리가 없어
아무도 너에게 귀를 귀울이지 않아
갈수록 어려워져 쉬워지지 않아

비록 세상은 널 외면하더라도
혼자서만 먼 길 돌아서 가더라도
절대 놓지마
뒤돌아 보지마
이건 혼자 만의 싸움
아직 포기마
자꾸 반복되는 일상의 감옥
숨쉬기도 빽빽한 수많은 과목
누구의 과욕때문에 이 지루한 가속은 계속돼?

Epik High – Breathe (Mithra's Word) *Translated by Ji-Su Park*

A dream is sweet.
Like a flower that blooms in spring after winter,
I smile after my struggle through the hard times.
Going against the gaze called 'society'
"Just quit it!"
My parents' pressure concerns me.
But the experience that the society really wants -- it is
a secret garden that one cannot find in the books.
The body feels it by itself
and the skin breathes.
It is a beautiful attempt, even though
hands and feet get blisters.
"I want my child to be more successful than me"
Pushing that heavy pressure to private academic institutions
It will be okay, as long as there's private tutoring.
"But why are my child's eyes losing the glow?"
Because what he wants to see are blocked;
because others pre-plan for his youth, his life.
Everyone is breathless;
everyone's tired of competition.
There is no space for the children to stand anymore.
Nobody listens to you
It gets harder and harder;
it doesn't get easy.
So you just gotta breathe…
Even if the world turns away from you
Even if you have to walk a long path all by yourself
Never give up,
never look back.
This is your fight
Don't give up, yet.
A prison within the constantly repeating daily life
Numerous subjects that make it
way too stuffy to breathe
Whose greed caused all this tedious acceleration?

온 몸에 퍼져만 간 독, 책상 앞에 앉으면 마비돼
재미가 없어
그물에 물처럼 답이 새
못하는게 죄라, 벌로 계속 달리게 만드니까 위축 돼
거부감은 히말라야 산이 돼,
성공을 말하면서 보여 줄 수 있는 거라곤
서로 넘어 뜨리고 짓밟고 싸워 욕질하는 정서?
아무것도 배울 것은 없어
그냥 귀를 열어 들어주면 돼
아닌 듯 해도 어깨에 손 올려주면 돼
무너져 갈 때 등에 날개 달아주면 돼
힘내라고 딱 한마디만 하면 돼
아무도 너에게 귀를 귀울이지 않아
갈수록 어려워져 쉬워지지 않아

비록 세상은 널 외면하더라도
혼자서만 먼 길 돌아서 가더라도
절대 놓지마
뒤돌아 보지마
이건 혼자 만의 싸움
아직 포기마
아무도 너에게 귀를 귀울이지 않아
갈수록 어려워져 쉬워지지 않아

My whole body is poisoned;
it gets paralyzed when I sit in front of a desk.
It's not fun.
The answer escapes
like water in a fishnet.
Incapability is a sin, never-ending running is a punishment;
I am intimidated and
my repulsion becomes the Himalayas.
What you can show while speaking of success
is only the sentiment of beating, trampling over
and fighting against each other?!
There's nothing to learn;
you just have to open your ears to listen.
You just have to put your hands on my shoulders
even if you are not sure about it.
You just have to put some wings
on my back when I'm collapsing
You just have to tell me, "You can do it"
Nobody listens to you
It gets harder and harder;
it doesn't get easy.
So you just gotta breathe…
Even if the world turns away from you
Even if you have to walk a long path all by yourself
Never give up,
never look back.
This is your fight
Don't give up, yet.
Nobody listens to you
It gets harder and harder;
it doesn't get easy.
So you just gotta breathe…
Breathe in,
Breathe out
Easy, so easy…

다이나믹 듀오 - 어머니의 된장국

나이는 갓 서른 외제차를 끄는
또래에 비해서 기름값 걱정을 덜하는
주변 사람들의 질투가 좀 심해서 높은 연봉에 관해선
언급을 안하는 그는
과도한 업무에 동창 모임에도 못 가
사치가 좀 심한 여자친군 달달 볶아
야근을 밥 먹듯 아침은 안 먹듯 하며 소화제를 달고 사는
더부룩한 날들
약간의 조증 폐쇄 공포증
혼자 뿐인 넓은 집
냉장고엔 인스턴트 식품
혀 끝에 남은 조미료 맛이 너무 지겨워
그가 간절하게 생각나는 건 바로...

Dynamic Duo – Mother's Soybean Paste Soup
Translated by Ji-Su Park

- Dynamic Duo, one of the most well-known hip-hop artists in South Korea, describes the busy lives of people working in the contemporary Korean society. Dynamic Duo illustrates how the busy modern-day people in Korea all miss their home and their mothers' Korean cooking, especially the delicious soybean paste soup. Mother's soybean paste soup is something that never changes.

Almost thirty-years-old, driving a foreign car:
compared to his peers, he doesn't have to worry
so much about the price of oil.
He doesn't mention his high income
because of his jealous neighbors.
He can't even go to school reunions
because of his excessive work.
His extravagant girlfriend nags him.
Frequent overtime night work and infrequent breakfast;
he lives in bloated days with digestants.
A little bit of mania and claustrophobia,
in a large house all by himself.
Instant foods in the fridge; he's sick of
the remaining taste of MSG on the edge of his tongue
What he truly craves is…

어어어어어어 어머니의 된장국
담백하고 맛있는 그 음식이 그리워
그 때 그 식탁으로 돌아가고픈
어어어어어어 어머니의 된장국
담백하고 맛있는 그 음식이 그리워
잠깐의 생각만으로도 배고픈
그의 나이는 이제 오십
한 달이 다 되어가, 떨어져 사는 가족들의 얼굴을 본지
한때는 돈 푼 꽤나 만졌던 그지만
지금 남은 건 빚 더미와 몸뚱이 뿐이야
집은 보증 잘못 섰다가 날렸지,
잘되던 사업은 욕심 부리다 망쳤지
아내와 자식에게 있을 때 못 해준 게 미안해
집에 못 가고 밤낮으로 일하네
배보다 더 휴식이 고픈 삶처럼 밥이 퍽퍽해 물 말아 먹는
오늘도 소주 한 병으로 저녁을 때우는 지친
그에게 필요한 건 바로...

Mother's soybean paste soup
Longing for that light, delicious dish,
wanting to go back to that dinner table back then
Mother's soybean paste soup
Longing for that light, delicious dish,
I already got hungry from thinking about it
He's now fifty years old.
It has been about a month since
the last time he saw his family away.
Back then, he used to deal with a lot of money;
but now, the only leftovers
are the debt and his body.
He lost his house by having underwritten somebody's debt,
ruined his thriving business by being greedy.
He feels sorry for not taking care
of his wife and children enough
when he had everything.
Now he can't go home but
works every day and night.
He craves for a break rather than food;
his life is like a bowl of dry rice that needs water.
Overwhelmed with fatigue,
he is having a bottle of soju for dinner today.
What he needs is…

어어어어어어 어머니의 된장국
담백하고 맛있는 그 음식이 그리워
그 때 그 식탁으로 돌아가고픈
어어어어어어 어머니의 된장국
담백하고 맛있는 그 음식이 그리워
잠깐의 생각만으로도 배고픈
서른이 되어가도 아니 그 후로도
더 더욱 그립기만 하겠죠
하나뿐인 그 맛
어느 새 내 혀 끝엔 침이 고여
어어어어어어 어머니의 된장국
담백하고 맛있는 그 음식이 그리워
그 때 그 식탁으로 돌아가고픈
어어어어이어어 어머니의 된장국
담백하고 맛있는 그 음식이 그리워
잠깐의 생각만으로도 배고픈
그녀는 나이에 비해서 조금 이르게 부모 품을 떠나
서울로 도망치는데
짧은 가방 끈이 조금 콤플렉스지만
야무진 꿈 하나만큼은 비만, 남보다 잠도 덜자
먼 훗날에 설 자리를 위해서는 몇 푼이라도 더 벌자
즐겨 듣는 음악 DJ DOC지만, 돈 좋아 명예 좋아

Mother's soybean paste soup
Longing for that light, delicious dish
I want to go back to that dinner table back then
Mother's soybean paste soup
Longing for that light, delicious dish
I already got hungry from just thinking about it

When I become thirty years old, no, even after that,
I will miss it even more – that unique taste –
and my mouth waters already.

Mother's soybean paste soup
Longing for that light, delicious dish
I want to go back to that dinner table back then
Mother's soybean paste soup
Longing for that light, delicious dish
I already got hungry from just thinking about it

She left his parents and ran away to Seoul
when she was still so young.
Her lack of education is her complex, but
her great dream is rich – for her dream,
she sleeps less than others.
For the place to stand in future,
she has to earn even a little more.
Her favorite music is DJ DOC, but
money and reputation she likes.

못생겨도 능력있는 남자가 좋아
주위에 남자들은 말발만 좋아
사투리를 아직 못 감추니
직장에선 촌스러운 까투리
외로움을 반찬으로 혼자 먹는 밥은 지겨워
서울의 삶, 그리고 간은 좀 싱거워
타향 생활이 너무 힘겨운 그녀에게 필요한 건 바로
어어어어어어 어머니의 된장국
어어어어어어 어머니의 된장국
어어어어어어 어머니의 된장국
어머니의 된장국이 그리워...

She likes men with skills,
even though they're ugly.
But men around her can only talk well.
She can't hide her countryside dialect yet, so she's
treated as a country hen pheasant at work.
She's sick of eating rice
with loneliness as a side dish;
she's tired of her life in Seoul – it's just
not seasoned enough.
Her life away from home is tough, and
what she needs is…

Mother's soybean paste soup
Mother's soybean paste soup
Mother's soybean paste soup

We all miss our mothers' soybean paste soup…

Catullus 9
Gaius Valerius Catullus

Verani, omnibus e meis amicis
antistans mihi milibus trecentis,
venistine domum ad tuos penates
fratresque unanimos anumque matrem?
venisti! o mihi nuntii beati!
visam te incolumem audiamque Hiberum
narrantem loca, facta, nationes,
ut mos est tuus, applicansque collum
iucundum os oculosque saviabor.
o, quantum est hominum beatiorum,
quid me laetius est beatiusve?

Catullus 9
By Gaius Valerius Catullus
Translated by Carolyn Tobin

Veranius, standing before all
my 300,000 friends to me,
have you come home to your household gods
and harmonious brothers and old mother?
You have come! Oh, what blessed news for me!
I will see you safe and hear your stories of Spain,
The places, deeds, peoples,
As is your custom, and grasping your delightful neck
I will kiss your mouth and your eyes.
Oh, out of all the most blessed men,
who is happier or luckier than I?

Catullus 101
Gaius Valerius Catullus

Multas per gentes et multa per aequora vectus
advenio has miseras, frater, ad inferias,
ut te postremo donarem munere mortis
et mutam nequiquam adloquerer cinerem,
quandoquidem fortuna mihi tete abstulit ipsum,
heu miser indigne frater adempte mihi.
nunc tamen interea haec, prisco quae more parentum
tradita sunt tristi munere ad inferias,
accipe fraterno multum manantia fletu
atque in perpetuum, frater, ave atque vale

Catullus 101
By Gaius Valerius Catullus
Translated by Carolyn Tobin

After passage through many peoples and many seas
I come to these wretched funeral rites, brother,
to give you the last gift to the dead
and to speak to your silent ashes in vain,
since fortune has torn you away from me,
poor brother stolen from me undeserving.
But meanwhile these things, which by an old custom of our
    ancestors
are handed down at funerals, a sad gift—
Accept them sodden with a brother's tears.
And so always, my brother, hail and farewell.

Catullus 68 a
Gaius Valerius Catullus

Quod mihi fortuna casuque oppressus acerbo
conscriptum hoc lacrimis mittis epistolium,
naufragum ut eiectum spumantibus aequoris undis
sublevem et a mortis limine restituam,
quem neque sancta Venus molli requiescere somno
desertum in lecto caelibe perpetitur,
nec veterum dulci scriptorum carmine musae
oblectant, cum mens anxia pervigilat,
id gratum est mihi, me quoniam tibi dicis amicum
muneraque et Musarum hinc petis et Veneris.
sed tibi ne mea sint ignota incommoda, Manli,
neu me odisse putes hospitis officium,
accipe quis merser fortunae fluctibus ipse,
ne amplius a misero dona beata petas.
tempore quo primum vestis mihi tradita pura est,
iucundum cum aetas florida ver ageret,
multa satis lusi; non est dea nescia nostri
quae dulcem curis miscet amaritiem:
sed totum hoc studium luctu fraterna mihi mors
abstulit. o misero frater adempte mihi
tu mea tu moriens fregisti commoda, frater,
tecum una tota est nostra sepulta domus,
omnia tecum una perierunt gaudia nostra,
quae tuus in vita dulcis alebat amor.
cuius ego interitu tota de mente fugavi
haec studia atque omnes delicias animi.
quare, quod scribis Veronae turpe Catullo
esse quod hic quisquis de meliore nota

Catullus 68a by Gaius Valerius Catullus

Translated by Carolyn Tobin

That you have been oppressed by fortune and a bitter fate
you send to me in this letter written with tears,
so that as a shipwreck tossed out from the foaming waves of the sea
 I might raise you up and restore you from the very threshold of
    death,
whom sacred Venus does not abide to rest in sweet sleep
left behind in a bachelor's bed,
nor do the muses of ancient authors delight with their sweet song
when your anxious mind remains awake.
I am pleased, since you call me a friend
and you look to me for the gifts of the Muses and of Venus.
But lest my troubles are unknown to you, Manlius,
and you think that I hate my duty as a friend,
realize that I have been dipped in the waves of fortune myself,
and seek the gift of solace from someone less wretched.
Ever since the time when the toga of manhood was first given to
    me,
when my budding age drove sweet youthful spring,
it was pleasing enough to play; the goddess was not unknown to me
who mixes the sweet bitterness of cares:
but the death of my brother stole away all my zeal with grief.
Oh brother, taken from wretched me,
you in dying have shattered my good fortune, brother,
and you hold buried with you all of our home,
all of our joys have perished with you,
which your sweet love sustained in life.
Since your death I have fled with my whole mind
these studies and all the delights of the soul.
When you write that it is unseemly for me to be in Verona
because here anyone of the better sort

frigida deserto tepefactet membra cubili,
id, Manli, non est turpe, magis miserum est.
ignosces igitur, si, quae mihi luctus ademit,
haec tibi non tribuo munera, cum nequeo.
nam quod scriptorum non magna est copia apud me,
hoc fit quod Romae vivimus: illa domus,
illa mihi sedes, illic mea carpitur aetas;
huc una ex multis capsula me sequitur.
quod cum ita sit, nolim statuas nos mente maligna
id facere aut animo non satis ingenuo
quod tibi non utriusque petenti copia parta est:
ultro ego deferrem, copia si qua foret.

can warm their chilled limbs on my deserted couch,
this, Manlius, is not unseemly, but rather the greatest of sorrows.
 Therefore you will forgive me if, I do not provide these gifts for
     you
which sorrow has taken from me, since I am unable.
For there are actually not very many poems here with me,
since I live in Rome: she is my home,
she is my dwelling, there my years are spent;
only one small book-box of many has followed me here.
Since this is the way it is, I don't wish for you to establish hateful
     thoughts in your mind
that there is not enough desire in my natural mind to do this
because I do not have much of what you sought:
I would have sent them already, if they were available.

Lebai Malang
Raja Haji Yahya

Al kisah, maka adalah sebuah desa. Maka didalam rantau itu adalah seorang lebai pandai mengaji dan taat ibadatnya kepada Allah ta`ala, istimewa pula perangainya tersangat adab dan santun, serta dengan tulus ikhlas hatinya kedua laki isteri. Ia itu tinggal disebuag dusun.

Sekali peristiwa, datanglah seorang laki-laki kerumahnya mengajak akan dia melawat orang mati. Maka kata Pak Lebai, baiklah. Kembalilah tuan dahulu,. Dan seketika lagi datang pula seorang kanak-kanak menjemput Pak Lebai kerana hendak kenduri berkhatam pengajian. Maka jawab Pak Lebai, yalah, baliklah engkau dahulu. Ada sekejap pula datang seorang lagi mempersilakan Pak Lebai keterataknya oleh hendak berdikir kenduri Maulud. Maka itu puj disanggup juga Pak Lebai, demikianlah juga katanya. Maka ketiga-tiga mereka itu pun pulanglah kerumah masing-masing berhadirkan sekalian alatnya kerana harapkan Pak Lebai akan datang juga kerumahnya.

Hatta, dinanti-nantilah oleh semua pemanggil itu akan Pak Lebai beberapa lamanya hingga beralih matahari, tiadalah juga Pak Lebai datang. Maka yang mati itu pun dimandikan serta disembahyangkan lalu ditanamkan. Dan demikian juga yang berkhatam itu pun dikhatamkan oranglah dan yang berkenduri itu pun bertampillah berdikir, masing-masing dengan pekerjaannya.

Kelakian, maka tersebutlah perkataan Pak Lebai. Kemudian daripada mereka yang ketiga itu telah kembali, maka ia pun sembahyang zuhur. Sudah sembahyang lalu berfikir didalam hatinya, kemana baik aku pergi ini? Jika aku pergikepada orang mati tentu aku mendapat sedekah kain putih dan tikar.

"The Unlucky Mister Turban"
Malay Oral History recorded by Raja Haji Yahya
Translated by Eileen Chen

As the story goes, there was a village. In that village was a turbaned man who was well-versed with the Quran, and was diligent in his religious duties, and was especially polite and courteous, and was sincere and truthful with his wife. This couple lived in an orchard.

One day, a man came to his home and asked him to preside over a funeral. And Mister Turban said, yes I will, now you may go back to where you came from. A while later came a child who invited him to a banquet celebrating a boy's completion in reading the Quran. And Mister Turban said, yes, now you go home. And later came someone with an invitation to another reception, thrown in honour of the Prophet. And Mister Turban said, yes yes yes. So all three callers went back to their homes and prepared themselves for Mister Turban's arrival, believing that he would arrive soon.

The hosts waited for Mister Turban until noon, but he never showed up. So the funeral-goers bathed the dead man, said their prayers, and then buried him. The boy who completed the Quran was celebrated and praised as he deserved; while the guests of the Prophet's reception went ahead with their chanting and singing. Business went on as usual, without Mister Turban.

So what about Mister Turban? When all of the three house-callers left, Mister Turban went to pray. After his prayers he considered carefully: which of the three should I attend? If I go to the funeral I will be presented with bale of white cloth and a mat.

Dan kalau aku pergi kepada orang berkhatam pengajian itu, perutku tentulah kenyang, dan sedekah pula secupak daging kerbau, serta kelapa setali dan kampit beras satu. Dan jikalau aku pergi kepada orang berdikir itu perut aku tentulah kenyang makan lempeng penganan angkatan orang itu. Maka kalau begitu, baiklah aku pergi kepada orang mati itu dahulu, kerana sabda junjungan dahulukan kerja wajib daripada kerja yang lain-lain.

Hatta, telah Lebai Malang berfikir demikiaan, maka ia pun pergilah kerumah orang yang kematian itu. Dengan takdir Allah ta`ala Pak Lebai bertemu dengan orang-orang yang pergi menanamkan orang mati itu baru pulang sahaja dari kubur. Maka kata saudara si mati, Allah, Pak Lebai, mengapa lambat datang? Sudahlah apa boleh buat? Tiada hendak menjadi rezeki saya.

Maka Pak Lebai pun pergilah pula kerumah orang berkhatam itu. Serta ia sampai kesana, orang semuanya habis hendak balik. Demi dilihat oleh orang empunya kerja itu, katanya, ah, ah ini pun Pak Lebai baru sampai. Mengapa Pak Lebai lambat datang? Sekarang apa pun tiada lagi, semuanya telah habis, melainkan barang dimaafkan sahajalah hal saya ini, kerana semuanya telah habis sekali.

Maka kata Pak Lebai, tiada mengapa, asalkan sudah selamat, sudahlah. Kemudian ia pun berjalan menuju kerumah orang bermaulud itu. Setelah ia sampai kesana, orang baru lepas berangkat saja, masing-masing orang pun hendak kembalilah. Maka apabila dilihatnya oleh tuan rumah akan Pak Lebai, maka katanya, Allah mengapa lambat datang Pak Lebai? Hingga penatlah saya menanti tiada juga Pak Lebai sampai. Kemudian diperbuatlah mana-mana yang dapat. Naiklah, Pak Lebai, nah inilah yang ada hanya sebungkus penganan saja lagi, lain semuanya sekali telah habis.

If I go to the boy's celebration, I will get a full stomach from the feast, and will also be given a cup of mutton, a string of coconuts and a sack of rice. And if I go to the Prophet's receptions I will be stuffed full with flat cakes. Taking everything into consideration, it is best that I attend the funeral first, because God's words had told him to put obligatory duties before other pursuits.

Off he went to the funeral place. On his way he saw the funeral-goers, who were on their way back from the graveyard, done with the burial. One of them said, God, Mister Turban, why did you come late? It's no matter, what else can we do about my lateness? Maybe it is not my fortune to be able to bury him with you.

So Mister Turban went to the house where the boy's celebration was held. When he arrived there, the guests were already packing, ready to leave. They saw him and said, Ah ah, so this is Mister Turban, who was just arriving. Why did he come late? There's nothing left now, everything is gone, except for the unwanted goods.

And Mister Turban said, it is no matter, all is good, as long as everything went according to plan. After that he headed towards the Prophet's reception. The banquet was just ending when he arrived, and everyone was ready to head home. When the host saw Mister Turban, he said, God why did you arrive late? I've waited painfully and you never showed up. So he went looking for something he could give to Mister Turban. Here, Mister Turban, this packet of fried cake is the only thing left, everything else is gone.

Maka ujar Pak Lebai, tiada mengapa apa pula yang disusahkan saya ini. Lalu diambilnya bungkusan lempeng itu serta berjalan pulang kerumahnya. Kelakian, maka hari pun hampir petang Pak Lebai pun sampailah kekampungnya lalu teringatlah ia akan air niranya diatas pohon kabung tiada berambil lagi. Maka ia pun pergilah kepohon kabung itu dan lempengnya itu pun disangkutkannya pada singai tempat iaa memanjat pohon itu. Maka Pak Lebai pun sampailah kepada bacuk niranya itu. Dilihatnya bacuk itu penuh berisi air nira.

Dengan takdir Allah, lempengnya yang ditinggalkannya dibawah itu sudah digonggong oleh anjing, dibawanya lari. Maka setelah dilihatnya oleh Pak Lebai akan hal penganannya itu digonggong oleh anjing, maka hilanglah fikirannya, lalu ia mencabut goloknya serta dipunggaikannya kepada anjing itu, tiada kena. Dan diambil bacuk nira yang penuh dengan nira itu, lalu dibalingkannya, tiada juga kena. Maka ia pun terjun dari atas pohon itu berkejar sekuatnya menghambat binatang bedebah itu.

Maka oleh tersangat pantasnya Pak Lebai mengejar anjing itu hingga terkepunglah ia, tiada tentu arahnya hendak lari lagi, istimewa pula hari sudah malam buta. Maka anjing itu pun masuklah kedalam lubang batang kayu bersembunyi membawa bungkusan kuih yang separuh sudah dimakannya sambil lari itu. Maka Pak Lebai pun sampailah kepada tempat anjing itu menyembunyikan dirinya. Dicarinya kayu tiada, dan lain-lain benda pun tiada juga hendak disumbatkannya pada lubang itu. Maka Pak Lebai pun oleh tersangat berang hatinya, lalu menanggalkan seluar dan baju serta songkoknya, lalu disumbatkannya kepada lubang itu. Maka Pak Lebai pun tinggal bertelanjang bulat sahaja. Maka sianjing sial itu pun keluarlah lari mengikut lubang yang sebelah lagi yang tiada bertutup itu, mengonggong bungkusan itu dengan pantasnya masuk kedalam hutan lalu hilanglah sekali tiada kelihatan pada mata Pak Lebai.

197

And Mister Turban replied, it's no matter, don't trouble yourself. But he took the packet anyway and then headed home. It was nearing afternoon when he reached his village, and he was reminded of the Sugar Palm sap that he hasn't collected yet from the tree. So to the tree he went; he hung his packet at a nearby branch, and then climbed up the tree. He was pleased to find that his collecting cup was filled to the brim with sweet sap.

As fate would have it, a dog came by and snuck away the packet of fried cake that he left under the tree. When Mister Turban saw this, he lost his mind. He took out his machete and hurled it at the dog, but he missed it. Then, madly, he flung his cup at the dog, throwing all the sweet sap into the air, yet still he missed the dog. Undaunted he leapt from the tree to the ground and chased after the dog with all his might.

Mister Turban was a quick man on foot; he managed to corner the dog. The dog, already half-blind from the impending nightfall, was now trapped. So he hid himself in a hollow tree trunk with the half-eaten packet of fried cake. Mister Turban looked around for bits of wood to plug the end of the trunk, to no avail. With anger burning in his head, Mister Turban took off his clothes and his turban, and stuffed them into the tree trunk. There he was, stark naked in the middle of the woods. The dastardly dog found a way out through the other unplugged end of the trunk; with the food packet between its teeth, it dashed quickly into the woods without being noticed by Mister Turban.

Maka Pak Lebai pun tercengang-cenganglah mengintai anjing itu kesana kemari.

Hatta seketika lagi terbanglah dua ekor burung punai betul-betul menuju Pak Lebai, kerana pada sangka burung itu tunggul kayu, oleh Pak Lebai bertelanjang bogel, seurat benang pun tiada lekat pada tubuhnya. Setelah dilihat oleh Pak Lebai akan punai itu datang, ia pun segeralah mengadakan lengannya dan membukakan kedua ketiaknya. Maka punai itu pun betullah masuk kedalam lubang ketiaknya, seekor disebelah kiri hendak menangkap burung itu. Wah apabila dirasa oleh burung itu badanya sudah tiada terapit lagi, maka keduanya pun terbanglah naik keatas pohon kayu yang berhampiran disitu. Setelah dilihat oleh Pak Lebai punai itu terbang, putihlah matanya dengan putus asanya kerana segala pekara yang diusahakannya itu suatu pun tiada memberi faedah kepadanya.

Maka ia pun mengucapkan syukurlah kepada Allah lalu ia pun kembalilah kepada lubang kayu tadi hendak mengambil kain bajunya. Sekunyung-kunyung suatu pun tiada lagi, sudah diambil oleh orang. Maka pergi pula ia kepohon kabung mencari goloknya dan bacuk niranya, semuanya telah ghaib, suatu pun tiada lagi. Wah apatah lagi, sesal Pak Lebai pun tiadalah berguna lagi, lalu teringatlah ia akan bidalan orang tua-tua, kalau secupak, takkan segantang, rezeki sudah sebanyak itu.

Maka Pak Lebai pun naiklah kerumahnya. Telah dilihat oleh isterinya Pak Lebai bertelanjang bogel itu, marahlah ia, seraya katanya, kena apa awak demikian ini, seperti laku orang gila? Kemana pergi seluar dan baju awak? Maka oleh Pak Lebai diceritakannya segala hal ehwal yang telah berlaku keatas dirinya. Maka Mak Lebai pun naiklah radangnya, seraya mengambil kayu api, disesahkannya kebelakang Pak Lebai seraya berkata:

So Mister Turban stood huffing, looking for the dog.

Soon a pair of pigeons came flying towards him – Mister Turban was nude without a thread on his body, and looked like a tree stump. As soon as he saw the pigeons Mister Turban flung his arms wide open and exposed his armpits. The pigeons got caught in his armpits! Mister Turban raised his right arm to grab the pigeon in his left armpit; but when both pigeons felt the pressure loosening in his armpits, they immediately took flight and escaped onto a nearby tree. Mister Turban sighed in disappointment of all his efforts – none of what he did brought rewards.

Still he gave thanks to God, and went back to the hollow tree trunk to retrieve his clothes. Alas there was nothing there! They have already been stolen. He retraced his steps to the Sweet Palm, looking for his machete and his sap-collecting cup; but none of them were to be found. Wrought with regret, Mister Turban thought of an old-man's saying: if it's a handful, it won't become a bucketful, because that is all it was meant to be.

So Mister Turban returned home. His wife, appalled with his nudity, yelled angrily, Why are you acting like a madman? Where have all your clothes gone to? So Mister Turban recounted everything that happened to him that day. Missus Turban lost her temper and threw firewood on Mister Turbans back, all the while lamenting:

'Lebai nasib langkahan malang , Kehulu hilir penat berulang Celaka sial bedebah jembalang Pakaian dibuang bertelanjang pulang.'

Maka Pak Lebai pun lari masuk kedalam kelambu mencari kain, lalu duduk termenung memikirkan halnya yang telah jadi, serta dengan berangnya sebab penat dan sakit kena bahan oleh kayu api Mak Lebai. Lalu ia bersyair pula:

'Ayuhai nasib fikir miskin, Dapat sedekah sebungkus lempeng, Habis hilang baju dan kain, Penganan habis dibaham anjing.

Penat berkejar tidak terkira, Kesana kemari tersera-sera, Punah golok bersama nira, Pulang kerumah mendapat mara.'

Maka demikianlah ceritanya Pak Lebai Malang itu, adanya

Mister Turban whose path was damned,
To and fro with haste he went,
Hapless cursed dastardly and lame,
Nude and cold he was homeward sent.

So Mister Turban ran into his chamber looking for clothes, and sat dazed thinking about his day, the burns on his back still fresh and stinging. And then he sang:

This is the fate of the poor,
A packet of cakes he gets,
But gone are his clothes and threads,
While a dog devours his loot.
And he has to run after,
Here, there, till his mind tires,
Extinct were his Sap and knife
While a fiery welcome awaits at home.

So this is the story of Mister Turban.

٧ آن لقمه که در دهان نگنجد بطلب

وان علم که در نشان نگنجد بطلب

سریست میان دل مردان خدا

جبریل در آن میان نگنجد بطلب

Jalal al-Din Rumi (1207-1273) was a Persian Sufi poet. He settled and produced most of his works in Konya, where his shrine is today. The following is a poem from the collection *Say Nothing*.

Translated by Aisha Dad

Yearn for that morsel that cannot be grasped in thought
Yearn for the wisdom that cannot be grasped in definition
That secret hidden in the hearts of men of God
That which even Gabriel, yearning, cannot grasp.

مگّے گیاں گل مکدی ناہیں
بھانویں سو سو جمعے پڑھ آبے

گنگا گیاں گل مکدی ناہیں
بھانویں سو سو غوطے کھابے

گیا گیاں گل مکدی ناہیں
بھانویں سو سو پنڈ پڑھ آبے

بلھا شاہ گل تانیوں مکدی
جدوں میں نوں دلوں گوابے

پڑھ پڑھ عالم فاضل ہویا
کدے اپنے آپ نوں پڑھیا ای نئیں

جا جا وڑدا مندر مسیتے
کدے من اپنے وچ وڑیا ای نئیں

اویس روز شیطان نال لڑداں
کدے نفس اپنے نال لڑیا ای نئیں

بلھا شاہ اسمانی اڈائیاں پھڑدا
جیڑھا گھر بیٹھا انہوں پھڑیا ای نئیں

Bulleh Shah (1680-1757) was a Punjabi Sufi poet from the Punjab area in modern day Pakistan. His tomb is in Kasur.

An excerpt from the Punjabi Sufi poetry of Bulleh Shah:
Translated by Aisha Dad

Going to Makkah is not enough
Even though hundreds of prayers are offered

Going to Ganga is not enough
Even though hundreds of cleansings are done

Going to Gaya is not enough
Even though hundreds of holy verses are recited

Bulleh Shah, it is only enough
When the "I" from my heart is lost

Reading, he became a scholar
Yet he never read himself

Often he enters temple and mosque
Yet he never entered into his own Self

In vain everyday he fights with Satan
Yet his own ego he never fought

Bulleh Shah grasps for celestial flights
Yet the one sitting at home he never grasped

Константин Симонов

Жди меня, и я вернусь.
Только очень жди,
Жди, когда наводят грусть
Желтые дожди,
Жди, когда снега метут,
Жди, когда жара,
Жди, когда других не ждут,
Позабыв вчера.
Жди, когда из дальних мест
Писем не придет,
Жди, когда уж надоест
Всем, кто вместе ждет.

Жди меня, и я вернусь,
Не желай добра
Всем, кто знает наизусть,
Что забыть пора.
Пусть поверят сын и мать
В то, что нет меня,
Пусть друзья устанут ждать,
Сядут у огня,
Выпьют горькое вино
На помин души...
Жди. И с ними заодно
Выпить не спеши.

Жди меня, и я вернусь,
Всем смертям назло.
Кто не ждал меня, тот пусть
Скажет: - Повезло.
Не понять, не ждавшим им,
Как среди огня
Ожиданием своим
Ты спасла меня.
Как я выжил, будем знать
Только мы с тобой,-
Просто ты умела ждать,
Как никто другой.

Wait for me by Konstantin Simonov
Translated by Lela Jgerenaia

Wait for me, I shall return
If you only wait, longingly enough
Wait, when the sulphureous rain
Brings you sorrow
Wait when the snow falls heavily
Wait when it's burning hot
Wait, when others cease to wait,
Yesterday quite forgotten.
Wait, when no letters come
From far away
Wait, when patience fails
Amongst those who wait with you.
Wait for me, I shall return
Don't wish well to those
Who feel in their heart
It's time to forget.
Though mother and brother believe
That I no longer exist
Though friends weary of waiting
Seated by the fire
Drinking sour wine
To the memory of my spirit...
Wait. Do not rush
To drink with them.
Wait for me, I shall return,
Despite all fatality.
Let those who refused to wait for me,
Choose to say: 'His luck was good',
Those who failed to understand, failed to wait.
As if from the flames
By your waiting
You have saved me.
Only we two will know
How I survived –
It will simply be that you knew how to wait
Like no other.

О Пушкине

Трудно сказать что-нибудь о Пушкине тому, кто ничего о нем не знает. Пушкин великий поэт. Наполеон менее велик, чем Пушкин.

И Бисмарк по сравнению с Пушкиным ничто. И Александр I и II, и III просто пузыри по сравнению с Пушкиным. Да и все люди по сравнению с Пушкиным пузыри, только по сравнению с Гоголем Пушкин сам пузырь.

А потому вместо того, чтобы писать о Пушкине, я лучше напишу вам о Гоголе. Хотя Гоголь так велик, что о нем и писать-то ничего нельзя, поэтому я буду все-таки писать о Пушкине.

Но после Гоголя писать о Пушкине как-то обидно. А о Гоголе писать нельзя. Поэтому я уж лучше ни о ком ничего не напишу

Даниил Хармс. 1936.

Daniil Kharms
About Pushkin (1936)
Translated by Genia Nizkorodov

It's difficult to say anything about Pushkin to those who know nothing about him. Pushkin was a great poet. Napoleon was not as great as Pushkin.

And Bismark, compared to Pushkin, was nothing. And Alexander the I, the II, and the III were just bubbles[7] compared to Pushkin. Everyone compared to Pushkin is a bubble, but compared to Gogol, Pushkin himself is a bubble.

And so instead of writing about Pushkin, it would be better for me to write about Gogol. Yet Gogol is so great, that nothing can be said about him... So I had better write about Pushkin after all.

But after talking about Gogol, it seems rude to write about Pushkin. Yet it's impossible to write about Gogol. Therefore, it's better that I don't write about anyone at all....

---

[7] "bubble" is a direct translation
In modern Russian, the word used is a slang for airhead

Fácil palabra
De Hugo Lindo

1

Fácilsería la palabra
sin hojas.
Fácil como un vacío.
Como una sombra.
Pero ocurre al contrario: te arrimas al silencio
y ella te acosa
llena de ideas,
de memorias,
siempre con algo entre las manos.
Y simplemente no la logras
desnuda, sola.

4

Teníamosquedecirnosmuchascosas
y no hallábamoscómo.
Era mejorasí.Corría el tiempo
y envejecíamos con él.
Y eso era hermoso.
Porquepensandoapenas, o sintiendo y pensando,
o nada mássintiendo,
adivinábamos
lo quees el zumo de estetestimonio:
teníamosquedecirnosmuchascosas,
pero¿cuáles?
¿Y cómo?

11

Amor amoramoramor setenta veces,
setenta veces siete veces.
Amor amoramoramor. Nadie habrá que lo olvide.
Siemprequién lo recuerde.

The word would be easy by Hugo Lindo

Translated by Hattie Arevalo

1

The word would be easy
without leaves.
Easy as emptiness.
Like a shadow.
But the opposite happens: you get closer to silence
and the word harasses you
full of ideas,
of memories,
always with something in her hands.
And you simply never get her
naked, alone.

4

We had to say many things
and we couldn't find how to do it.
It was better that way. Time flew by
and we aged with it.
And that was beautiful.
Because barely thinking, or feeling and thinking,
or just feeling,
we guessed
what the essence of this truth is:
that we had to say many things,
but which ones?
And how?

11

Love lovelovelove seventy times,
Seventy times seven.
Love lovelovelove. None shall forget it.
Always someone to remember it.

"Hadithi za Kimasai/ Contes et Lègendes maasai." Eric Fayet and Ruckya Sanatu-Basseporte

Hapo zamani za kale aliishi bibi kizee wa kimasai kwenye boma pamoja na watoto wake na wajukuu. Bibi huyu alikuwa mzee sana kiasi kwamba alikuwa hawezi kutembea tena. Kufuatana na tabia za kabila la kimasai kuhama sehemu moja kwenda nyingine kwa ajili ya kutafuta malisho ya mifugo yao, watoto wake waliokuwa wanamtunza waliondoka wote kwenda mbali na boma; hivyo wakamwacha bibi kizee peke yake kwenye kibanda. Walifanya hivyo kwa kuwa sehemu hiyo haikuwa na majani ya malisho ya ng'ombe. Sababu hiyo iliwafanya wahame kwenye maeneo hayo na kutafuta maeneo yaliyo na maji na majani. Hata hivyo walimwahidi bibi kizee kuwa watakuwa wanawatuma watoto wadogo ambao hawajaweza kuchunga mbuzi kwenda kumjulia hali bibi yao na kumpelekea chakula kila siku.

Kila siku watoto walipokaribiakufika kwa bibi yao walikuwa wakiimba wimbo huu, "Bibi bibi sisi ni watoto wa watoto wako tumekuja kukutembelea." Bibi kizee naye aliitikia, "Ingieni ingieni ndani, maadamu bado ninaishi." Tabia hii ni ya wajukuu kwenda kumjulia hali bibi yao iliendelea kwa muda wa mwezi mmoja hivi. Kwa bahati mbaya siku moja muda wa usiku, simba alipita kwenye maeneo ya kibanda cha bibi kizee. Akanyata na kuelekea kwenye kibanda na kuchunguza, akafanya hivyo kwa muda wa siku mbili, akajua mazingira yote ya pale, jinsi wale watoto wanavyokuja kumwona bibi kizee huyo na wimbo wanaouimba kabla ya kuingia kibandani. Siku iliyofuata simba huyo aliingia ndani ya kibanda cha bibi kizee na akamvamia na kumla bibi kizee huyo. Baada ya kumla alikaa humo ndani kwenye kibanda mpaka asubuhi.

Maasai Stories
By Eric Fayet and Ruckya Sanatu-Basseporte
Translated by Jacqueline T. Killenga

Once upon a time there lived an old Maasai lady with her children and grandchildren. This lady was so old that she was unable to walk any longer. As per the culture of the Maasai tribe to move from one place to another in search of pasture for their livestock, her children had to go away from home, leaving her alone in their hut. There was no more grass for the cattle near the compound hence they immigrated to other areas to find water and grass. However, they promised the old lady that they would send the children, too young to graze goats, to go see her and bring her food every day.

Each day when the children approached their grandmother's hut, they sang this song, "Grandmother grandmother we are the children of your children and we have come to visit you." The grandmother responded, "Enter enter inside, as long as I still live." This behaviour of the grandchildren going to see their grandmother continued for a month or so. Unfortunately, one day at night, a lion passed near the grandmother's hut. He sneaked towards the hut and explored the surroundings. He did this for about two days and became familiar with the environment, and how those children came to see the old lady including the song they sang before entering the hut. The next day the lion went into the grandmother's hut, seized and ate her. After feeding on the grandmother, the lion stayed in the hut until morning.

Siku iliyofuata wajukuu walimtembelea bibi yao kama ilivyokuwa kawaida yao. Walipokaribia kwenye kibanda cha bibi yaowaliimba wimbo wao.

"Bibi bibi sisi ni watoto wa watoto wako tumekuja kukutembelea." Humo ndani simba akasikia wimbo huu. Wakati huo wanya ma wote walikuwa wanazungumza lugha za kibinadamu. Kwa kuwa simba alishakariri sauti ya yule bibi kizee, kwa hiyo aliposikia wale watoto wakiimba aliitikia kama alivyokuwa akiitikia yule bibi kizee.

Akaitikia "Ingieni ingieni ndani, maadam bado ninaishi." Wale watoto walipoingia ndani simba aliwakamata na kuwala wote.

The next day the children visited their grandmother as usual. As they approached the grandmother's hut they sang their song.

"Grandmother grandmother we are the children of your children and we have come to visit you." The lion heard the song. At that time, animals could speak human languages. As the lion knew how to immitate the voice of the grandmother, when he heard the children singing he responded in the same manner as the grandmother did.

He said, "Enter enter inside, as long as I still live." When the children entered inside the hut, the lion caught them and ate them all.

Mke wa Mpiganaji

Contes et Légendes Maasaï – Hadithi za Kimaasai

Hapo zamani za kale, kabla wazungu hawajafika Afrika, wapiganaji wa Kimaasai wa kijiji kimoja walienda katika mapigano. Mmoja kati yao alichukua kibuyu cha maziwa kasha akamwambia mke wake, "Unayaona haya maziwa? Yaweke vizuri ukae karibu nayo tena usiyanywe; nikiwa hai huko kwenye mapambano, maziwa haya utayaona meupe – nikiwa nimekufa utayaona yamegeuka kuwa mekundu." Kisha mume wake akaondoka kwenda kwenye mapigano ya kikabila. Kila siku, kila saa, wakati wote, mchana na usiku, msichana huyo mdogo aliangalia kwenye kibuyu cha maziwa kwa wasiwasi. Alikuwa akimpenda sana mumewe.

Wiki moja baadaye, usiku mmoja wakati fisi alipokuwa akilia mbali kidogo, bahati mbaya ilimwangukia: maziwa yalikuwa yamegeuka kuwa mekundu. Kwa kukata tamaa aliyamwaga maziwa hayo kwenye kibuyu kingine akajitayarisha kwenda kumtafuta mume wake. Alipokuwa njiani, alikutana na kikundi cha wapiganaji, akaanza kuimba, "Mmemuona mume wangu? Yuko wapi? Yuko wapi? Mkuki wake ni mrefu, sime yake ni kali na imechongoka; kuna manyoya ya mbuni kichwani kwake. Ni kijana mwenye uzuri wa sura, mrefu, mwenye nguvu na ana macho meusi, makali."

"Nenda ukaulize kikundi kinachofuata, watakueleza zaidi," walimjibu. Walikuwa hawapendi kumueleza ukweli halisi. Ukweli ni kwamba aliuawawa na wapiganaji wenzake wa kijiji kimoja. Mke huyo alingoja kikundi kilichofuata kasha akaanza kuimba tena, "Mmemuona mume wangu? Yuko wapi? Yuko wapi? Mkuki wake ni mrefu, sime yake ni kali na imechongoka; kuna manyoya ya mbuni kichwani kwake. Ni kijana mwenye uzuri wa sura, mrefu, mwenye nguvu na ana macho meusi, makali."

217

The Warrior's Wife
Translated by Sylvia

A long time ago, before the white man came to Africa, some Maasai warriors from one village were going for a tribal battle. One among them took a gourd full of milk and told his wife, "You see this milk? Keep it beside you always and don't drink it; as long as I am alive during the fight this milk shall remain white. If I am dead, it will turn red." Then he left for the battleground. Every day, every hour, day and night, the young wife would peer into the gourd worriedly for she loved her husband dearly.

One week later, on a night when the hyenas were howling in the distance, bad luck befell her: the milk had turned red. Out of despair, she poured the milk into another gourd and prepared herself to go look for her husband's body. On the way, she met a group of other warriors and began to sing, "Have you seen my husband? Where is he? Where is he? His spear is long, his sword is sharp; he wears ostrich feathers on his head. He is a handsome young man, tall and strong with intense dark eyes."

"Go and ask the next group, they will tell you more," they told her. They didn't want to tell her the truth, which was that he had been killed by warriors from his own village. The wife waited for the next group that followed, and started singing again: "Have you seen my husband? Where is he? Where is he? His spear is long, his sword is sharp and he wears ostrich feathers on his head. He is a handsome young man, tall and strong with intense dark eyes."

Mpiganaji ambaye alikuwa kama chifu wa mapigano alimuonesha mti,

"Unauona huo mbuyu?"

"Ndio!"

"Unaona hao ndege wanaoruka angani?"

"Ndio," mke alijibu tena

"Hapo utampata mume wako."

Kwa kweli ndege hawakuwa na kitu chochote bali mwonekano wao uliashiria ishara mbaya.

"Mmemuona mume wangu?" aliuliza tena, akikimbia mpaka kwenye mbuyu. Akamuona mume wake amelala chini ya mti akikaribia kufa. "Mpenzi wamekuua?" alimuuliza mumewe kwa huzuni. "Ndio!" alieleza, kwa sauti ya mbali. Mkewe akafungua kibuyu na kuyamwaga maziwa juu ya tumbo la mumewe, kwenye jeraha na vidonda vyake.

"Unaweza kunibeba, mtu ninayekaribia na kufa?" mpiganaji alimuomba mke wake, lakini kwa bahati mbaya hakuweza kumnyanyua. Alimburuza mpaka kwenye boma ambalo hakulijua. Wenye boma walimpoona jinsi mpiganaji alivyokuwa ameumia na kuwa na majeraha mengi, walimuuliza mkewe, "Amefanya nini huyu?"

Mke akawajibu, "Amepigwa na wapiganaji wenzake!"

"Wako wapi sasa?"

"Sijui chochote!" alijibu mke.

Baada ya kumuuliza maswali mengi, walimchukua kama ulivyo ukarimu wa Wamaasai kwa mtu mwenye hali hiyo. Walimweka kwenye chumba chenye giza na utulivu; walichinja ng'ombe na kuchoma nyama yake – lakini sehemu zote zenye mafuta waliziweka kwa ajili ya mgonjwa. Baada ya wiki chache, kutokana na matibabu mazuri, mpiganaji aliweza kusimama mwenyewe. Kutokana na chakula chenye nguvu, akapona na kubadilika;

The warriors' leader showed her a tree.

"Do you see this baobab tree?"

"Yes!"

"Do you see those birds flying around it?"

"Yes…"

"There you shall find your husband."

The birds were a bad omen.

"Have you seen my husband?" The young woman ran towards the baobab tree. She saw her husband lying beneath it, dying.

"My love, have they killed you?" she asked her husband with sadness.

"Yes!" he responded in a faint voice.

She opened a gourd of milk and poured it over his wounds.

"Will you be able to carry me, a dying man?" he asked his wife, but unfortunately she was unable to lift him. She thus dragged him to a nearby *boma* (homestead) where she didn't know anyone. The people there, upon seeing her husband's grave injuries, asked her "What has happened to him?"

She replied, "He has been struck by his fellow fighters!"

"Where are they now?"

"I know nothing of their whereabouts!" the wife replied.

After asking her several questions, they took him in. The Maasai are a generous people; they put him in a quiet, dark room from him to rest. They slaughtered a cow and roasted its meat – but saved all the fatty parts for the patient. After a few weeks, thanks to the care he received, the warrior was able to stand up on his own. He had gained strength from the good food;

akafanya mazoezi magumu sana na kuwa mwenye nguvu hata kuliko alivyokuwa mwanzo. Aliwashukuru wale watu waliomtibu.

Alipeleka mifugo kule kwa marafiki zake waliomtibu. Akaenda tena mara ya pili, na mara ya tatu. Alipata mifugo mingi sana aliyoteka. Siku moja aliwaambia marafiki zake kuwa anataka kurudi nyumbani, yeye na mke wake na vitu vyake alivyopata kwenye mapigano; uamuzi wake ulijadiliwa kwenye kikao cha wenyeji wake. Kundi la wanyama alilokuwa amepata kwenye mapigano liligawanywa sehemu mbili sawa; wenyeji wake wakambariki wakisema, "Nenda kwa amani, sasa hakuna mtu atakayeweza kukuumiza tena."

Walipokaribia kufika kwao, mpiganaji na mke wake, walikutana na mtoto mdogo. Mpiganaji akamtuma kwa baba yake kumueleza ya kuwa yeye anarudi. Alipokuwa anaingia kijijini, kila mtu alishangaa kwani walidhani amekufa. Aliwaalika watu wote wa kijiji kwenye hafla kubwa, wakiwemo wale waliojaribu kumuua. Alitoa damu kwa ajili ya kunywa, nyama ya kula an baadhi ya mifugo kwa ajili ya kugawana na wanakijiji. Wanawake waliimba na kucheza, morani waliruka. Siku hiyo ilikuwa ya furaha sana, na sherehe ilichukua siku nzima.

Jioni, kila mtu alirudi kwenye boma lake. Wapiganaji waliokuwa wamejaribu kumuua pia walienda kwenye vitanda vyao kulala, wakiwa wameshiba na wenye furaha. Usiku ule ule, wapiganaji wale walianza kutapika damu. Hawakushangazwa sana na hali hii iliyowafanya hatimaye wafe, kwani walikuwa wamekula chakula kutoka kwa mtu waliyejaribu kumuua – mtu ambaye asingerudia tena uzima wake kama sio mapenzi ya mke wake.

he exercised vigorously and became even stronger than before. He was very grateful to the people who had nursed him.

He took a herd of livestock to the hospitable family. And more, a second and third time. One day, he told these new friends that he wanted to return home, with his wife and war booty. His decision was discussed by his hosts' council of elders. They then divided the herd of all the animals he had accumulated into two equal herds, gave him one lot, and blessed him saying, "Go in peace; now nobody will be able to harm you again."

When he and his wife neared their home, they met a young child. The warrior sent the child to go and tell his father that he was returning home. As they entered their village, everyone was amazed as they had thought that he was dead. They could not believe their eyes and some even collapsed when they saw him.

He invited all the villagers, including those who had tried to kill him, to a huge feast. He set out blood to drink, meat to eat and even some livestock to share with the villagers. The women sang and danced, the young *moran* warriors leapt high into the air. It was a very happy occasion and the celebration lasted all day long.

In the evening, everyone returned to their *boma*. The warriors who had tried to kill him also went to bed, full and happy. Later that night, those warriors began to vomit blood and eventually died. Yet they were not surprised by this condition, for they had accepted food from a person whom they had attempted to kill – somebody who would not have regained his life had it not been for his wife's love.

علم و عشق

علم نے مجھ سے کہا عشق ہے دیوانہ پن
عشق نے مجھ سے کہا علم ہے تخمین و ظن
بندہ تخمین و ظن! کرم کتابی نہ بن
عشق سراپا حضور، علم سراپا حجاب!
عشق کی گرمی سے ہے معرکہء کائنات
علم مقام صفات، عشق تماشائے ذات
عشق سکون و ثبات، عشق حیات و ممات
علم ہے پیدا سوال، عشق ہے پنہاں جواب!
عشق کے ہیں معجزات سلطنت و فقر و دیں
عشق کے ادنیٰ غلام صاحب تاج و نگیں
عشق مکان و مکیں، عشق زمان و زمیں
عشق سراپا یقیں، اور یقیں فتح باب!
شرع محبت میں ہے عشرت منزل حرام
شورش طوفاں حلال، لذت ساحل حرام
عشق پہ بجلی حلال، عشق پہ حاصل حرام
علم ہے ابن الکتاب، عشق ہے ام الکتاب!

223

- **Sir Muhammad Iqbal** (1877-1938), more famously known as Allama ("Scholar") Iqbal, is the most renowned and revered Philosopher-poet of the East. He was from Lahore. He wrote both in Urdu and Persian. The following is a translation of the Urdu poem "Ilm o ishq" (Doctrine and Passion) from the collection called *The Rod of Moses,* published in 1936.

"Doctrine and Passion"
By Muhammad Iqbal
Translated by Aisha Dad

Doctrine whispered to me, "Passion is foolishness!"
Passion whispered to me, "Doctrine is approximation and guess,
O man of approximation and guess! To become a bookworm do not press.

   Passion is absolute presence, Doctrine an absolute veil,
From the heat of Passion exists the commotion of the universe,
Doctrine is the destination of measures, Passion a vision of substance,
Passion peace and eternity, Passion cause and terminus

   Doctrine is questions already begot, Passion is answers concealed!
Miracles of Passion are nobility and mysticism and faith,
Humble slaves of Passion are possessors of crowns and wealth
Passion is both house and dweller, Passion both time and earth

   Passion is absolute belief and belief the lighted trail!
On the way of Love a comfortable destination is *haram*[8]
Tempest of a storm *halal*,[9] pleasure of the shore *haram*
Lightning on Passion *halal*, attainment of Passion *haram*

   Doctrine is the progeny of a book, Passion the mother of a book!"

---

[8] Haram is something that is forbidden and proscribed.
[9] Halal is something that is approved and encouraged.

Vội Vàng
- Xuân Diệu –

Tôi muốn tắt nắng đi
Cho màu đừng nhạt mất;
Tôi muốn buộc gió lại
Cho hương đừng bay đi.
Của ong bướm này đây tuần tháng mật;
Này đây hoa của đồng nội xanh rì;
Này đây lá của cành tơ phơ phất;
Của yến anh này đây khúc tình si.
Và này đây ánh sáng chớp hàng mi;
Mỗi sáng sớm, thần vui hằng gõ cửa;
Tháng giêng ngon như một cặp môi gần;
Tôi sung sướng. Nhưng vội vàng một nửa:
Tôi không chờ nắng hạ mới hoài xuân.
Xuân đang tới, nghĩa là xuân đang qua,
Xuân còn non, nghĩa là xuân sẽ già,
Mà xuân hết, nghĩa là tôi cũng mất.
Lòng tôi rộng, nhưng lượng trời cứ chật,
Không cho dài thời trẻ của nhân gian,
Nói làm chi rằng xuân vẫn tuần hoàn,
Nếu đến nữa không phải rằng gặp lại.
Còn trời đất, nhưng chẳng còn tôi mãi,
Nên bâng khuâng tôi tiếc cả đất trời;
Mùi tháng, năm đều rớm vị chia phôi,
Khắp sông, núi vẫn than thầm tiễn biệt...
Cơn gió xinh thì thào trong lá biếc,
Phải chăng hờn vì nỗi phải bay đi?
Chim rộn ràng bỗng đứt tiếng reo thi,
Phải chăng sợ độ phai tàn sắp sửa?

Hurriedly
- Xuan Dieu –
Translations by Ngoc Pham

I want to turn off the sun,
So it won't dim all the colors.
I want to hold the wind tight,
So all the scents will stay.

Bees and butterflies, it is the honey season.
Look, Here blossoms of the green fields,
For leaves to dance on young limbs,
For the swallows and orioles, there is a love song.
And here the lights flashing the eyelashes.
Each morning, knock knock! - it's the god of happiness.
January is tasty, just like a close lip.
I am happy, but hurried by half.
I never wait for summer to miss spring.

Spring is coming, meaning spring is leaving.
Spring is young, meaning it is getting older.
Spring is over, meaning I will pass away.
My heart is wide, but god is thrifty.
Not letting the youth stay for long.
No points in speaking, spring is still periodic.
There is no second young time.
Heavens and earth still there, but there is no more me.
So I am sorry for both heavens and earth,
Month and year smell the taste of farewell,
All rivers and mountain whisper the pain of parting.
The pretty wind whisper inside the leaves.
Is it because it has to go?
Busy birds suddenly stop cheeping.
Are they scared they will soon fade?

Chẳng bao giờ, ôi! chẳng bao giờ nữa...
Mau đi thôi! mùa chưa ngả chiều hôm,
Ta muốn ôm
Cả sự sống mới bắt đầu mơn mởn:
Ta muốn riết mây đưa và gió lượn,
Ta muốn say cánh bướm với tình yêu,
Ta muốn thâu trong một cái hôn nhiều
Và non nước, và cây, và cỏ rạng,
Cho chếnh choáng mùi thơm, cho đã đầy ánh sáng,
Cho no nê thanh sắc của thời tươi;
- Hỡi xuân hồng, ta muốn cắn vào ngươi!

Never, oh! never again….
Let's go, it is not twilight yet,
I want to hug,
The whole new life seems to just begin:
I want to chase the swinging clouds and winds,
I want to feel high with the butterflies and love.
I want to enjoy the deep kiss.
And natures, trees and grasses..
To be groggy the scent, to be full with lights,
And to be full with beauty of freshness.
   - Hey pink spring, I want to bite you.

Made in the USA
Lexington, KY
26 August 2011